Radical Economics

General Editor: SAM AARONOVITCH

Debates between economists are not just technical arguments amongst practitioners but often reflect philosophical and ideological positions which are not always made explicit.

Discontent grew with the prevailing economic orthodoxy as the long period of economic expansion in the advanced capitalist economies came to an end in the 1970s; disenchantment was expressed in open discussion about the 'crisis' in economics and in the rise of various kinds of radical economic theory, often using the general title of 'political economy'.

Many economists have looked for a more fruitful point of departure in the ideas of Marx and the classical economists and also in such contemporary economists as Kalecki and Sraffa. Although it is possible to identify a broad radical stream, it does not mean that there are no significant controversies within this radical approach and, indeed, it would be unhealthy if this were not the case.

Can radical economic theory interpret the world better than the current orthodoxy which it challenges? And can it show also how to change it? This is a challenge which this series proposes to take up, adding to work already being done.

Each book will be a useful contribution to its particular field and should become a text around which the study of economics takes place.

Radical Economics

Monopoly Capitalism

KEITH COWLING

Professor of Economics at the
University of Warwick, Coventry, England

First published 1982 by
THE MACMILLAN PRESS LTD
London and Basingstoke
Companies and representatives throughout the world

ISBN 0 333 29204 9 (hard cover)
ISBN 0 333 29205 7 (paper cover)

Printed in Hong Kong

Contents

Acknowledgements

Serious work on this book began in Cambridge during a sabbatical in 1978—9, and I am much indebted to Bob Rowthorn for extended discussion over that period and since. I hasten to add that he does not agree with all my analysis. Sam Aaronovitch, Paul Geroski and Norman Ireland have read carefully through the whole manuscript and made useful comments and corrections. Shirley Patterson, Ann Sampson, Kerrie Beale and Yvonne Slater did all the typing. I am grateful to all of them.

University of Warwick   Keith Cowling
Coventry, England
February 1981

1
Introduction

This book aims at an analysis of some of the major features of contemporary capitalism. It was inspired by the work of Kalecki (1938, 1939 and 1971a), Steindl (1952) and Baran and Sweezy (1966), but it neither agrees with all that they say nor attempts to cover precisely those issues which they attempted to cover. The book sets out to explore the division of national income between workers and capitalists in a world where monopoly or oligopoly capitalism dominates, both for its intrinsic interest and because of its relevance for the process of accumulation in capitalist society. It will be argued that the major corporations are now organised in, often interlinked, oligopoly groups, in many cases with an international base, and have captured dominant positions which are relatively unassailable. They will remain unassailable partly because these dominant oligopolies will invest in their maintenance in order to secure the benefits of the stream of monopoly profits associated with their position. Competition between and within national oligopoly groups will occasionally break out, but these should be seen as transient elements in the accommodation of different capitals to each other. The norm in such an oligopolistic world will be collusion over output or pricing policies, with collusion itself being the product of potentially rivalrous behaviour — a seemingly paradoxical result which we will seek to substantiate in Chapter 2. Agents have substantial economic power and will use it in a variety of ways which has to be recognised in any discussion of the distribution of national income. With this end in view Kalecki's model of distribution will be completed with the derivation of the relationship between elements of market structure and the share of gross capitalist income plus salaries in value-added (Chapter 2). This will allow the precise identification of those processes which lead to changes in the share of profits in national income. Having done this we will then recognise that although the degree of monopoly may change as market structure variables change, this need not imply that the aggregate level of profits will have changed since it will be partly determined by the level of aggregate output (Chapter 3). The variable which allows the adjustment of a changing degree of monopoly to a given level of aggregate profits is the degree of capacity utilisation. Thus, although increases in the degree of monopoly will imply an underlying tendency for the share of profits to rise, the actual level of profits, and therefore the rate of return on capital, will also be determined by the level of effective demand working through the rate of capacity utilisation.

One of the components of effective demand is the consumption of capitalists, but in a world of managerial capitalism consumption out of profits comes to be concentrated more and more within the corporation rather than outside it. For this reason, and because under managerial control management will extract a portion of what should be regarded as profits as its own pecuniary and non-pecuniary income, profits as measured in the accounts will tend to understate their true level. Two basic struggles can be identified within this context: one between big capital and small capital, where big capital tends to be represented internally and takes part in these internal consumption activities, and one between high-level and lower-level management (Chapter 4).

Class struggle between workers and capital, and its consequences for distribution and the rate of profit, will be identified in the context of a monopoly world (Chapter 5). It will be argued that workers as a class cannot easily raise their share of national income in such a world. However, to the extent that the processes of class struggle lead to a wage—price spiral then this is likely to lead to political intervention which will result, in the short term, in a reduction of both profit share and the rate of profit through the creation of excess capacity. Questions of class struggle must also lead to questions of international 'competition' (Chapter 6). This was the central theme of Glyn and Sutcliffe (1972), where they argue that British capital has been squeezed in recent years between the anvil of worker pressure and the hammer of international competition. In contrast we will argue that rising international trade in manufactures in a world of monopoly capital can increase the competition for jobs without increasing competition among capitalists. This can come about where dominant corporations have a substantial degree of control over imports, either via the intra-firm trade of transnational corporations, or via agency or franchise arrangements or distributional control over imports at wholesale or retail levels.

Such ramifications of the development of monopoly capital will be explored by examining the post-war development of the UK economy, making some brief comparisons with the US economy (Chapter 7). It will be argued that although the post-war histories of European and American capital have been qualitatively different they are tending towards convergence. European capital has possessed underlying dynamic forces which the USA has not possessed, but these are now dying out, so the full implications of the creation and development of the monopoly phase of capital, which have become evident in the USA, will now also become clearer within the European context. They will also be increasingly revealed by the fact that these economies are now operating under post-Keynesian rules — just as they were revealed under the pre-Keynesian rules of the inter-war period. This leaves capitalism with a tendency to stagnation, partly because of its monopolistic character, but also because of its reluctance to accept Keynesian policies because of their dynamic implications for the balance of power between capital and labour. The book closes with a brief analysis of an alternative economic and political strategy in the face of the current capitalist crisis.

No attempt has been made to provide an exhaustive treatment of monopoly capitalism. The analysis largely ignores detailed questions of the labour process under monopoly capital, but these get a good airing in Braverman (1974) and Friedman (1977). I have also avoided getting embroiled in the wider social implications of monopoly capital raised by Baran and Sweezy (1966). Perhaps more importantly I have largely avoided issues of imperialism, an extension to the analysis which I hope to work on in the near future.

2
Oligopoly and the Share of Profits

This chapter is concerned with the relationship between the degree of monopoly, defined as the mark-up of price on marginal cost, and the distribution of income, setting on one side for the moment issues of realisation, managerialism, worker pressure and international competition. However, since we are interested in demonstrating the extent of capitalist control over the degree of monopoly, and thus over the distribution of income, we will be concerned to isolate those factors which determine the degree of monopoly. We will in fact derive a specific link between different elements of market structure and behaviour — concentration, the degree of collusion and the price elasticity of demand — and the degree of monopoly by assuming profit-maximising behaviour on the part of each member of the oligopoly group. We will then assess the extent to which these elements of market structure are themselves within capitalist control. This will necessitate an examination of the extent to which the degree of monopoly is conditional on potential entry into the market by new rivals. Our analysis will suggest that the price—output decisions of the oligopoly group are essentially independent of potential entry but that the capacity decision may not be.

Having determined the extent to which capitalists are able to control the evolution of the degree of monopoly in specific industries, we will then aggregate over all industries and derive the implications of the aggregate degree of monopoly for the share of profits plus overheads in national income. This derivation will reveal that the level of imports entering the domestic monopolised production and distribution system will also affect the distributive shares.

The perspective on income distribution established in this chapter is heavily influenced by the work of Michal Kalecki (1938, 1939 and 1971a). In contrast to the dominant neo-classical view which assumed perfect competition and full employment and derived income shares in terms of the parameters of the production function, Kalecki saw the industries of the advanced capitalistic economies as being essentially monopolistic or oligopolistic and operating normally under conditions of excess capacity. This implied that price would exceed marginal cost, and marginal cost could reasonably be assumed to be constant within the normal range of output. Assuming, then, that marginal cost comprises the cost of wage labour, the ratio of price to marginal cost will define the ratio of profits plus overheads to wage bill, and the degree of monopoly (the ratio of price minus marginal cost to price) will define the share of profits plus overheads in value-added. Thus the aggregate share of profits plus overheads, and therefore the share of wages, in national income will be defined by the average degree of monopoly.[1] Forces leading to a high average degree of monopoly will imply a lower wage share and thus a higher share for profits and overheads.

Market Structure and the Degree of Monopoly

One of the major problems with Kalecki's analysis of the distribution of income in terms of the degree of monopoly was that it left the degree of monopoly itself undetermined, and therefore we will turn first to this question.[2] Since oligopoly is the general case under contemporary capitalism,[3] with some sectors effectively monopolised at the national, regional or local level, we will be determining the industry mark-up of price on marginal cost (the Lerner/Kalecki degree of monopoly or oligopoly) in terms of the structure of the industry in question and the effective recognition by the firms in the industry of their mutual interdependence.

Assuming that a fixed number of firms follow profit-maximising rules in the production and sale of a homogeneous product, equation (2.1) provides a useful way of describing industry equilibrium (see the appendix to this chapter for details of its derivation):

$$\frac{p_k - c_k{}'(X_k)}{p_k} = \frac{\alpha_k}{\eta_k} + \frac{(1 - \alpha_k)}{\eta_k} H_k \tag{2.1}$$

where p_k is the market price, $c_k'(X_k)$ defines the industry's marginal cost function, which is a weighted average of the marginal cost functions for the n firms in the industry, H_k is the Herfindahl measure of concentration $(\Sigma_i [X_{ik}/X_k]^2)$, η_k the absolute value of the industry price elasticity of demand $(- d \log X_k / d \log p_k)$, and α_k captures each firm's expectations about the response of each rival to its own output decision $([dX_{jk}/dX_{ik}] [X_{ik}/X_{jk}])$. These expectations could be different for each firm, in which case α_k could be loosely interpreted as the weighted average of such expectations.

Thus the degree of monopoly is directly related to the degree of concentration in the industry and inversely related to the absolute value of the industry price elasticity of demand. It is also affected by the value of α. The Cournot model of oligopoly behaviour assumes that each member of the oligopoly group takes the output of rivals to be fixed and invariant to their own output and therefore specifies a value of zero for α. Despite the existence of interdependence each firm assumes it away in setting its own output. This lack of recognition of interdependence puts a lower bound on the set of outcomes under oligopoly, with $[p - c'(X)]/p = H/\eta$. This is a point which is often lost sight of in discussions of oligopoly. The absence of collusion does *not* imply a competitive outcome. The outcome, in terms of the degree of monopoly, will still be conditional on the degree of concentration (H) and the industry elasticity of demand (η). Thus in oligopolistic markets where firms are proceeding quite independently to fix output, without either overt or tacit collusion, profit-maximising behaviour within such constraints can still ensure an output departing substantially from competitive output. For instance, a *non-collusive*, symmetric duopoly will have an equilibrium mark-up of price on marginal cost of one-third where the industry elasticity of demand is two. This is not to say that this is the expected outcome in the case of symmetric duopoly since, in the absence of external constraints, it is possible for the participants to do better than this. It should however be regarded as a lower bound, and a lower bound which departs farther and farther from the competitive outcome as the industry becomes more concentrated.[4]

The joint profit-maximising solution, $[p - c'(X)]/p = 1/n$, implies a value for α of unity, which establishes the upper bound on price-cost margins. The actual value of α can therefore be used as a measure of the degree of apparent collusion (see Cubbin, 1975b); $\alpha = 0$ implying zero collusion, $\alpha = 1$ implying perfect collusion, $0 < \alpha < 1$ implying some degree of imperfect collusion.[5] Equation (2.1) can then be interpreted as a convex combination of monopoly (perfect collusion) and Cournot (non-collusive) equilibria.[6] Whether the particular oligopoly equilibrium ends up close to the monopoly or Cournot positions will depend on the extent to which they can co-ordinate their output policies. We will delve into this question below, but before we do that we need to consider the generality of the result we have obtained.

Clearly the description of oligopoly equilibrium which has been developed above is general in the sense that it spans the whole range of possibilities between full and zero collusion.[7] It is less than general in that it assumes that all participants have essentially the same view about interdependence. In contrast Saving (1970) derived a relationship between concentration and the degree of monopoly assuming a basic assymmetry between a dominant collusive group and a competitive fringe. It is the recognition by the dominant group of the supply function for output from the competitive fringe in coming to their own price—output decisions which sets this model apart from the one we have described above, and we must therefore ask whether this represents an additional and useful way of describing oligopoly equilibrium. It seems to me that this alternative approach should be rejected as a useful additional description on two counts; first as a description of a typical industry and second as a useful description of behaviour, even if such industry structures existed.

On the first point it would seem that where industry structures appear as described, the 'competitive' fringe is typically either producing a different product to that produced by the dominant group, with a low cross-elasticity of demand, or the product produced is essentially complementary, on either the demand side or the production side, to that of the dominant group. But even if we were to grant that such industry structures may exist, it does not mean they will persist. Where such models are deficient is in assuming that the supply function of the competitive fringe is a constraint about which the dominant group can do nothing. If this were so then it would be a misuse of the term dominance. If such a fringe existed and became a threat to the profitability of the dominant group then we would expect the dominant group to do something about it. One solution would be to buy out the fringe, a solution which would always be possible given the higher valuation put on the assets of such a fringe by the dominant group. Alternatively such a fringe could be eliminated by an array of aggressive policies, like predatory pricing. Obviously this would only be optimal for the dominant group if the eliminated fringe were not immediately replaced by another with similar characteristics. This question will be postponed until we take up the question of entry, but the dominant firm model is the static version of the dynamic limit-price model of entry, and for related reasons we will argue that the degree of monopoly remains normally unaffected by the conditions of entry because alternative action by the dominant group will tend to dominate.

One other restriction on the generality of the result is the assumption of profit-maximising behaviour, within a fairly narrow context. In the next section we will relax this rather informally to see how the pursuit of profit leads to the modification of those factors which have been shown to determine the degree of monopoly. We will however want to stick with the assumption of profit-maximising behaviour in price—output determination. This does not mean that we reject managerial theories of the firm but we will interpret them in distributional rather than allocative terms (see Chapter 4). Others believe that those firms which are price-makers follow simple rules of thumb for price-fixing rather than adopting profit-maximising rules. Thus to some 'full' or 'normal' measure of cost is added some mark-up, but the way in which the mark-up is determined is usually left undefined. This does not seem to be a very helpful line to follow, and there is plenty of evidence to suggest that the mark-up can vary quite widely in patterns which are quite consistent with profit-maximising behaviour. The widescale incidence of systematic price discrimination revealed in various Monopolies Commission investigations would suggest both the existence of monopoly power and pricing behaviour according to profit-maximising rules.[8] Similarly, widely differing mark-ups in supermarkets have been observed.[9]

Lastly, it is of course the case that our formulation relates specifically to firms poducing a homogeneous product, when in fact many markets are characterised by product differentiation. Whilst equation (2.1) still stands as a useful description of industry equilibrium it is obviously the case that some firms will be in a relatively dominant position in the market because of their past investment in an amalgam of product and marketing strategies. Thus price–cost margins can vary across firms operating in the same market, but we will be focusing mainly on changes at the industry level.

Capitalist Control over the Degree of Monopoly

The factors we have identified as determining the degree of monopoly in an industry are obviously partly determined by the actions of firms within the industry in question, in contrast to the view expressed by Johnson (1973), who seemed to feel that the degree of monopoly was purely determined by the behaviour of consumers, given that their tastes determine the elasticity of demand for the product in question. This is obviously wrong in that in the oligopoly case, which we take to be the general one, the degree of monopoly is determined by concentration and the degree of collusion, as well as by the elasticity of demand, but, also, the elasticity of demand is itself at least partly a variable within the control of the firms in question,[10] just as the degree of concentration and collusion are. In the case of concentration we can see the monopolisation of specific industries as being a long-term aim of capital allowing for the exploitation of workers via the market as well as in the process of production. This aim may be helped or hindered by particular technological innovations, but, given the objective, we can expect innovations to be biased in a direction favouring the aim of a more concentrated structure. Thus innovations implying scale economies or facilitating control of large organisations are likely to dominate innovations implying deconcentration and disintegration. Given that monopoly rents are available as prizes for capital, we can expect that the stream of innovations will reflect the pursuit of such prizes as well as the pursuit of efficiency in a social sense. Thus we can expect technical progress in capitalist society to contribute to the development of more concentrated market structures.[11]

The actual process of concentration could come about via differential growth or horizontal merger and will affect the degree of monopoly both directly and indirectly. Increases in the index of concentration (H) imply a rising lower bound on the degree of monopoly. That is, Cournot behaviour will imply an increase in the degree of monopoly as concentration increases, but increasing concentration will also make a move from Cournot equilibrium more likely since the costs of collusion are likely to be reduced as concentration increases (see, for example, Stigler, 1964). In Stigler's model α, the degree of collusion would be interpreted in a probabilistic sense.[12] Thus monopoly pricing would be stable if each member of the oligopoly group felt certain that its own secret price cutting would be immediately detected and would lead to instant retaliation. At the other extreme, if each oligopolist confidently felt that price cutting would not be detected, then price would only become stable at the Cournot level. Since the probability of detection of secret price cutting, via the monitoring of its impact on market share behaviour, will increase with the level of concentration,[13] price will tend to stabilise at the monopoly level in the case of concentrated industries.

To be realistic the whole system would have to be formulated in dynamic terms since the question is not simply will rivals retaliate, but when will they retaliate. The shorter the retaliatory lag, the more likely it is that the monopoly price will be chosen, since the transient gains from price cutting will be limited compared with the long-term losses associated with an equilibrium price below the monopoly level. As the retaliatory lag lengthens a point will be reached where the transient gains are substantial enough to encourage price cutting and therefore price will only stabilise at a level below the monopoly level. We will simply argue that a smaller, tighter oligopoly group will be one in which each member will not only assume that retaliation will be more likely than in a larger, more loosely knit group, but also that it will be swifter because of the greater awareness and sensitivity of each member of the group regarding the behaviour of other members. Thus the advantages of price cutting will tend to disappear in such groups and monopoly or near monopoly prices will tend to be stable. This view would be strengthened by the expectation that a smaller, tighter group would be more likely to have a common view of the world, which would be cemented by the relative ease of communication within such a group.

Thus rivalrous behaviour and collusion coexist and result from a high degree of concentration within a specific market. The closer the rivalry, the more immediate is the response to any attempt to secure an advantage, but the very immediacy of the expected response serves to maintain the degree of collusion — it makes a breakaway movement unprofitable. This reconciliation of intense rivalry with monopoly prices could cause a diversion of competitive behaviour into channels which may be either more difficult to detect or more difficult to respond to immediately, but the degree of monopoly will typically be sustained or even enhanced by such policies. Various types of 'product' and advertising competition would be cases in point.[14]

Obviously many factors other than concentration determine the degree of collusion, economic, social and technical, some of which are in the control of the firms involved.[15] Let us define them as a vector of variables, u, and write the equation for the degree of collusion as:

$$\alpha_k = \alpha_k (H_k, u_k) \tag{2.2}$$

where $\partial\alpha/\partial H > 0$. However, even if perfect collusion were attainable, the degree of monopoly would still be constrained by the industry price elasticity. A perfectly elastic demand curve would ensure that even a monopolist would have no monopoly power.

The basic question which now arises is to what extent are consumer wants or tastes determined exogenously to the capitalist system and to what extent are they determined by the actions of capitalists. Orthodox demand analysis takes tastes as exogenous and eschews any place for advertising in the determination of consumer behaviour. But clearly, firms collectively can reduce the price elasticity of demand by creating and sustaining wants, that is by creating psychological or even physiological dependence,[16] by means of advertising. The actual effect of advertising on the price elasticity of demand is not unambiguous, because informational advertising could result in higher price elasticities by making people more aware of price differences and thereby making them more sensitive in their response to price cutting, and this may be typical of much of advertising by some sectors of the retailing industry. But even in such cases, where advertising's short-term impact is to increase the price elasticity of demand and thereby reduce the degree of monopoly, in the long term we might expect it to enhance the degree of monopoly via its impact on concentration. Thus although the initial effect of advertising by, for example, Tesco may be to make consumers more sensitive to price differences, and thus to reduce the degree of monopoly, in the longer term its effect would likely be to secure or increase Tesco's dominant position, thus tending to raise the degree of monopoly. Advertising used as a competitive weapon in this way can therefore contribute to a longer-term modification of market structure favouring the giant firms in the industry.

However, as far as manufacturers are concerned, the evidence points the other way: advertising tends to encourage brand loyalty and buyer inertia, which leads to increasing insensitivity to price changes.[17] This would seem to be the general case — advertising is a characteristic of monopoly power and in turn sustains and enhances it. This is illustrated by the results of Comanor and Wilson (1967) for the USA and

Cowling *et al.* (1975) for the UK, which show quite convincingly that raising the level of advertising will tend to raise the degree of monopoly. This can be illustrated by reporting one of the estimated regression equations from Cowling *et al.* for a sample of eighty-eight companies operating in the food industry:

$$\ln \left(\frac{p_i - mc_i}{p_i}\right) = -5.916 + 0.501 \ln A_i + 0.194 \ln \Sigma A_k$$
$$(-6.018) \quad (16.883) \quad\quad (2.057)$$
$$+ 0.545 \ln \Sigma CR_{4k} \quad -0.120 \ln K_i$$
$$(2.842) \quad\quad (-1.133)$$
$$\overline{R}^2 = 0.854$$
$$F = 128.0$$
$$(t \text{ values in brackets})$$

where $(p_i - mc_i)/p_i$ is approximated by value-added minus wages and salaries plus depreciation (implying constant average production costs), for the ith firm over the period 1965–9; A_i is total advertising expenditure by the ith firm for the period 1965–9 ÷ 5; ΣA_k is the weighted sum of advertising expenditure in all food markets in which the firm sells, for the period 1965–9 ÷ 5; ΣCR_{4k} is the weighted sum of four-firm concentration ratios for the food markets in which the ith firm sells, and K_i is the average net assets of the firm, 1965–9.

Clearly the explanatory power of the equation is quite high, the advertising variables are significant and of the expected sign, as is the concentration variable.[18] The results give strong support to the view that the degree of monopoly is positively related to the level of advertising, and we infer from this that advertising tends to result in decreasing price sensitivity and therefore implies lower price elasticities of demand.[19] We regard this as the general result but, as we have already mentioned, the relationship can theoretically go either way. However, the vast bulk of advertising simply does not provide the sort of information that would lead to greater price sensitivity. We have already indicated that parts of retailing may be an exception but we have also pointed to a more concentrated structure as a likely outcome. Nevertheless, there are cases where it appears that advertising has indeed resulted in lower prices — well, at least one: the case of spectacles in the USA (see Benham, 1972). This is an interesting exception because it reveals that the case where advertising would tend to bring down the degree of monopoly is exactly the situation where advertising is outlawed by collective action of the sellers themselves. This has happened in the case of opticians in the UK and most states in the USA, and is true of other professions. In most other cases there is a general antipathy on the part of sellers to any sort of regulation of advertising, the usual argument being that it represents an attack on freedom.[20]

In addition to advertising there are a number of other determinants of the price elasticity of demand which either are unconnected with the activities of the firms themselves or are of an unsystematic nature. Two interesting and related phenomena may be mentioned — the tendency for price elasticities of demand to show a secular decline related to the increase in real incomes, which tends to result in the increasing importance of habitual behaviour (Houthakker and Taylor, 1970)[21], and the tendency for elasticities of demand to increase in depression periods as consumers become more sensitive to price differences (Harrod, 1936). We simply recognise these other possible determinants of the price elasticity of demand (η) by a variable v and write the equation as

$$\eta_k = \eta_k \ (A_k; v_k) \tag{2.3}$$

where generally we assume $\partial \mid \eta \mid / \ \partial A < 0$.

Potential Entry, the Degree of Monopoly and Excess Capacity

The question of the implication of potential entry for the exploitation of monopoly and oligopoly positions is crucial, since these positions do exist and constitute the norm, and much of conventional economics relies on this mechanism for achieving competitive behaviour — taking entry in the broadest sense to refer to either new firms entering a specific market, existing firms producing a new product which is a close substitute for rivals' existing product, or foreign firms entering a new national market.[22] Does the existence of such potential entry, and the reactions of firms to it, mean that positions of monopoly power are more apparent than real? Much of the literature on the entry question could lead either to such a conclusion, or, alternatively, to an assessment of the height of barriers to entry before the degree of monopoly could be determined. Our argument, based mainly on the work of Spence (1977), will be that the question of the degree of monopoly and that of entry can be seen as essentially separable, so that potential entry will not imply that price will fall below the lower bound dictated by Cournot behaviour in an oligopoly group with a fixed number of members.

The entry-limiting price literature, going back to Bain (1956) and Sylos-Labini (1962) in its static form, and developing more recently into an array of dynamic variants, is basically saying that the conditions for entry into the industry determine the degree of monopoly within the industry.[23]

With a competitive fringe and a homogeneous product, the static model implies competitive pricing by the existing group in the absence of barriers to entry, since to price above such a level would leave the existing monopoly or oligopoly group with zero sales. As soon as we move to large-scale entry, and/or introduce time into the analysis, then we will experience a move from competitive pricing, even in the absence of conventional barriers to entry.[24] In the case of large-scale entry the potential entrant can no longer assume that post-entry price will not deviate from pre-entry. Assuming that entrants expect existing firms to maintain their rate of output in the face of entry (the Sylos postulate, which is of course a Cournot assumption on the part of entrants), Modigliani (1958) revealed that entry would be conditional on the magnitude of scale economies, the elasticity of demand and the size of the market. With substantial scale economies, relatively inelastic demand and a limited market, expected post-entry price will deviate markedly from pre-entry price and therefore equilibrium price for the oligopoly group (i.e. the price consistent with zero entry) can show a significant departure from competitive price. We have argued earlier that monopolists and oligopolists have at least some control over the dominant technology and over consumer tastes, so we should see the Modigliani result as being a quite general and important one. Certainly, assuming large-scale entry rather than a potential competitive fringe would seem to be more descriptive of reality, and it should also be remarked that even if potential competitive fringes do exist they are potentially quite easily digested by dominant corporations.

The dynamic, entry-limiting pricing literature, which has shown substantial growth in recent years, assumes a potential competitive fringe, makes its rate of entry a function of the price chosen by the existing group and generates a wealth-maximising price trajectory for the group which decays over time, starting somewhere near the monopoly level and having competitive price as some lower bound at some point in the future (see, for example, Gaskins, 1971). The important point coming out of the literature is that the optimal rate of entry as far as the existing group is concerned (i.e. that rate of entry consistent with the maximum flow of discounted profits for existing firms) is not generally zero. The trade-off between profits today and profits tomorrow implies a price today above limit price, which will ultimately mean that profits tomorrow will be lower because of entry. The general principle is one of 'making hay while the sun shines'. Always to set a limit price will simply mean that profits which could have been made are being foregone, but this is not the end of this particular line of argument.

An alternative view of the reaction to potential entry implies the separability of the price—output decision of the existing group from the decision about what to do about entry. One recently articulated view is that of Spence (1977), who argues that a possible response to the entry problem by the existing group is to invest in excess capacity.[25] This will act as a deterrent to entry so long as it allows the existing group to raise its level of output faster than the prospective entrant would, and so long as the prospective entrant sees it that way. Since some entry lag can generally be expected it would seem reasonable to infer that excess capacity can be an effective deterrent. But the very irreversibility of investment in excess capacity is itself an important characteristic of an effective deterrent — it allows the existing group to express a commitment to the industry and thus provides a foundation for credibility. The central idea is that the prospective entrants' evaluation of the prospects after entry will be conditional on the existing groups' potential rate of output, rather than their actual rate. Since the potential rate exceeds the actual rate where excess capacity exists, the prospective entrant will assume that there will be a substantial gap between pre- and post-entry price and can be expected to modify its behaviour accordingly.[26]

Spence offers this hypothesis as an alternative to the entry-limiting pricing approach and suggests that there are some cases, for example differentiated products or uncertain costs, where the price signal can be an inefficient one.[27] But one can go further than this and argue that the creation of some degree of excess capacity, rather than some reduction in what would otherwise be the optimal price, will generally be the appropriate response to potential entry. The grounds on which it can be expected to do so represent an extension of the previous argument about 'making hay while the sun shines'. Limit pricing, of whatever sort, implies that output is higher (price is lower) than would have been the case if entry had been ruled out. The capacity response to entry implies that the potential rate of output diverges from the actual rate for the same reason. Provided the implications for entry are the same (or that price is an inferior signal), the excess capacity strategy will always dominate, because actual output will be at that level consistent with maximum profits (for a sustainable degree of collusion) in the absence of entry.[28] Entry-limiting pricing behaviour can now be seen as having a capacity consistent with a rate of output above the monopoly or oligopoly equilibrium level, and actually using it, whereas the excess capacity hypothesis implies that the extra investment will take place, but the usual monopoly or oligopoly restrictions on the rate of output will be maintained. Thus oligopoly price—output equilibrium, as defined by equation (2.1), and therefore the degree of monopoly, are separable from the question of entry.

This is obviously a crucial result and it needs to be examined more closely. As Spence points out, separability will be achieved so long as marginal cost is invariant to the level of excess capacity. This is obviously not necessarily the case, and excess capacity (induced by potential entry) could result in lower marginal costs and therefore lower prices. This would not of course necessarily change the degree of monopoly, which would remain conditional on the level of concentration, the elasticity of demand and the degree of collusion. This raises a second interesting point, that of the link between excess capacity and the degree of collusion. If the degree of collusion is essentially determined by the speed of reaction by the group to anyone cutting price, then the existence of excess capacity may tend to bolster collusion by making it clear to all participants that rivals can react immediately (see Waterson, 1976). It is possible therefore that the degree of monopoly can rise with the threat of entry, a result which turns the conventional wisdom on its head. Interestingly, Spence (1977), and indeed Steindl (1952), argued precisely the other way. They both saw the existence of excess capacity, planned in the case of Spence, unplanned in the case of Steindl, as making collusion within the existing group more difficult, and therefore tending to bring the degree of monopoly down. In the case of Spence this position is difficult to understand since the level of excess capacity exists because it provides a credible threat to potential entrants, and by extension it should equally well serve as a credible threat to any existing member of the group who is thinking about increasing output or cutting price. If excess capacity did not exist generally, then any member of the group could freely act to increase its market share without fear of immediate retaliation. Of course, unplanned excess capacity, with which Steindl is concerned, could perform the same function. Under conditions of close rivalry the members of the oligopoly group will quickly recognise that they cannot solve their mutual problem of excess capacity by competitive price cutting. This led Kalecki (1939) to suggest that in recessions the degree of monopoly will tend to rise rather than fall. In terms of our model this implies an increase in the degree of collusion in response to mutual adversity. This is precisely what Phillips (1961) and Williamson (1965) predicted in their behavioural theories of inter-firm organisations: there would be cycles in the degree of collusion, with increases in recession and decreases in boom.

If we return to the question of planned excess capacity arising from the threat of potential entry, it is clear that, despite the fact that some gains can be made by cementing or enhancing the degree of collusion within the existing group, the existence of excess capacity nevertheless represents a burden for the group. It implies that profit and rate of return on capital are below what they might have been. In some circumstances it may be possible to use this capacity without incurring the disadvantages previously outlined. The necessary preconditions would be those generally associated with price discrimination, that is, an ability to isolate markets with different elasticities, but with control over third-party transactions. Probably the most obvious example is the separate treatment of domestic and foreign markets (see Blattner, 1972). So long as the foreign market price is greater than marginal cost, profit can be raised by actually using excess capacity for this purpose — provided that the capacity can be switched to domestic production relatively costlessly. This would seem an interesting further insight into the ramifications of monopoly power. In an attempt to maintain their monopoly positions, monopolies or collusive oligopolies may be driven into investment in capacity which is ultimately used for production for dumping in foreign markets, the point being that this would happen despite the fact that such investment would appear unprofitable in the absence of the initial entry threat in the domestic market. One interesting consequence is that any positive association between concentration, and/or firm size, and export performance cannot be simply interpreted as a measure of the superior efficiency of monopolies or giant firms — it may just as easily indicate the existence of monopolies investing in excess capacity to secure their domestic positions and disposing of at least some of the extra potential output in foreign markets.

However, the preconditions for such price discrimination will not always be met, and in that case the threat of entry in a world of monopoly or oligopoly will simply imply waste. In his analysis Spence focuses on excess capacity mainly in terms of plant and equipment, but the idea can be generalised to include all types of investment which will secure a monopoly position. He also mentions advertising investment and the associated capital stock, customer loyalty,[29] and investment in retail outlets and the associated capital stock, the distribution network.[30] But research and development investment and patenting can also form part of excess capacity, and will, as such, comprise social waste. This obviously does not imply that all activity in these areas is wasteful, and indeed such investment can serve as an antidote to a potential realisation crisis following monopolisation (see Chapter3), but it does mean that in attempting to secure their monopoly positions, firms will invest in, say, R & D but, having done so, they will simply put the inventions on the shelf. On the arguments as outlined above this can be optimal for the monopolist or collusive oligopoly group. Mandel (1968) catalogues a long list of cases of suppression of technical progress by the big monopolies, including new lubricants (Monsanto and Standard Oil), synthetic rubber for thirteen years (Standard Oil), fluorescent lighting (General Electric and Westinghouse), various developments in steel-making by the big US steel corporations, and the Tucker car, a revolutionary design evolved after the Second World War and suppressed by the big US automobile producers. More recently Select Committee hearings reveal fascinating glimpses of the unexploited innovatory capacity of IBM.[31] Evidence from Dr H. R. J. Grosch revealed that IBM had an 'enormous shelf full of fancy items'; 'IBM has not used its full powers of research and development in the market place at all'; and 'Enormous reservoirs of knowledge are available there. I do not think it is necessary to have that much to be reasonably competitive.' All this suggests that protective R & D is probably a widespread and significant component of planned excess capacity aimed at maintaining and enhancing positions of monopoly power.

We can conclude from the above discussion that the appropriate response to potential entry, as seen by the monopolist or collusive oligopoly group. Mandel (1968) creation of some degree of excess capacity rather than some reduction in what would otherwise be the optimal price, consistent, in the oligopoly case, with a sustainable degree of collusion.[32] Thus the mark-up of price on marginal cost will be, at least indirectly, independent of the conditions of entry — although the capacity response to entry can itself affect the conditions under which the degree of monopoly is determined — but the rate of profit and the profit share, being affected by both the degree of monopoly and the magnitude of overhead (capacity) costs, will not remain independent of these entry conditions. The actual *degree* of excess capacity will be conditional on the benefits accruing to the existing monopolist or oligopolists from keeping other firms out, and the costs of doing so. The more successful the existing group is at generating excess profits, the bigger will be the incentive to keep others out and thus the more substantial will be the degree of excess capacity,[33] i.e. price will have to fall very substantially to deter entry where existing pre-entry price is high relative to the average costs of the prospective entrant.[34] This of course implies that for a given degree of monopoly ($[p - c'(X)]/p$) for the existing group, the level of excess capacity required to deter entry is also determined by the average cost of the prospective entrant, which will in turn be determined by scale economies and conventional barriers to entry like advertising 'goodwill'; but in so far as these represent investments by the existing group to secure some control over entry they will comprise part of excess capacity. We will therefore assume that the optimal degree of excess capacity rises with the degree of monopoly, and that, in turn, it will serve to sustain or enhance the degree of monopoly. This is because, as we have already argued, excess capacity will serve to maintain or increase the degree of collusion since it allows an immediate response to any attempt to increase market share, and the greater is capacity, the bigger is the potential response. Since we expect excess capacity to increase with concentration, the existence of potential entry tends to reinforce our earlier conclusion that rivalrous behaviour and apparent collusion coexist and result from a high degree of concentration. The degree of monopoly is also likely to be enhanced wherever more intensive advertising forms part of the response to potential entry, given that we expect the price elasticity of demand to be inversely related to the level of advertising.

Our general conclusion is that the degree of monopoly will not be affected by the threat of entry, except in so far as it is made more durable by the existence of a higher level of excess capacity than would otherwise be the case. However, the threat of entry, by stimulating the creation of excess capacity, will tend to reduce the level of profits.[35] Monopoly power, reflected in monopoly pricing, will remain, but at least some of the implicit profits will be used up in the process of maintaining the monopoly position itself. In so far as the corporations involved are members of a tight group, perhaps with an international base (i.e. entry is not by outsiders), then expenditures undertaken to maintain dominant positions within any national market will be minimised, but they will still exist because collusion is sustained by credible rivalry, and such expenditures will generally be required to maintain credibility.[36]

Having established that the threat of entry will have no impact on the degree of monopoly outside the context of the determinants identified in equation (2.1), we can now see that, in the case of constant marginal costs, the ratio of profits plus overhead costs to sales revenue in the kth industry will be determined by market structure and the degree of collusion among firms in that industry, and the split between profits and overheads will be partly determined by the level of excess capacity whether planned or unplanned. Rewriting equation (2.1) in terms of profit (π) and overhead (F) costs yields:[37]

$$\frac{\pi_k^* + F_k}{p_k\, X_k} = \frac{\alpha_k}{\eta_k} + \frac{(1 - \alpha_k)\, H_k}{\eta_k} \qquad (2.4)$$

This is the separable output equation for the industry in which capacity costs do not enter as a determinant. The degree of monopoly and the conditions of entry into the industry would then determine the optimal capacity for the oligopoly group. With blockaded entry, optimal capacity will provide a rate of output equal to output defined by equation (2.4); if entry threatens then optimal capacity will be greater than the capacity required to sustain this rate of output, and the difference will increase with the degree of monopoly. Equation (2.4) can therefore be interpreted as an *excess* capacity equation, with market structure and the degree of collusion determining the extent to which the capacity to produce is actually utilised. As we have already argued, it is possible to envisage a bigger capacity for the industry, induced by potential entry, raising the degree of monopoly by raising α or reducing $|\eta|$, but it is possible for output of the existing group to increase as a result of the threat of entry. This could be the case if in the absence of entry the industry were to move into long-run equilibrium with zero excess capacity. Consider the simple, but fairly realistic, case of constant operating costs (b) and constant capacity costs (β). Long-run marginal costs would then be $b + \beta$, but with excess capacity marginal cost would be b, even in long-run equilibrium. Thus output would be greater, with excess capacity induced by entry because in the long-run marginal costs would be lower. However, in the world with which we are dealing we expect excess capacity to be the norm, even in the absence of the threat of entry (see the next section). The threat of entry will serve to determine the degree but not the general existence of excess capacity. This means of course that potential entry is less likely to invoke capacity expenditures on the part of existing monopolies or oligopolies. The required excess capacity may already be there for other reasons, whether planned or unplanned. But, whether or not the long-run rate of output is affected by the capacity response to potential entry, the degree of monopoly in any short-run situation with excess capacity remains unaffected.

A related point which has often been raised in connection with Kalecki's work is that the degree of monopoly implied by profit-maximising behaviour at any time may be consistent with a rate of return on capital which implies exit in the long term. Recognition of such a possibility does not imply of course that overhead (capacity) costs should enter the determination of price—output policies at a specific point in time when capacity is fixed. Some economists have abandoned profit-maximising behaviour at this point and have included capacity costs in the pricing decision, (see, for example, Eichner, 1976). There seems to be no good reason for doing this. We will argue in Chapter 3 that even in a world of mangerialism, corporations will choose price—output policies to maximise profits. This does not mean that the capitalist will remain passive in the face of a degree of monopoly which yields an unsatisfactory return on capital. We have already mentioned that the degree of collusion among capitalists may be increased under adverse circumstances such as recession or slump. More generally the search for better established monopoly positions may be stimulated. In a more competitive world exit and entry would take place to equalise rates of return. In the world we have described entry will be severely curtailed, and exit, although still relevant to particular lines of activity, is less likely to occur in the case of the major corporations themselves given their capacity to diversify by takeover. Potential entry will of course still have an impact on the rate of return through its impact on the level of planned excess capacity.

Empirical Evidence

There is a long history of empirical investigation into the inter-industry and inter-firm variation in profitability using various measures of concentration and barrier-to-entry variables, but it is unfortunately not possible to discriminate adequately between the competing hypotheses concerning the impact of potential entry. The real distinction between the two is that in the case of the limit-price hypothesis the degree of monopoly varies with the threat of entry, for a given level of concentration, degree of collusion and elasticity of demand, whereas in the case of the excess-capacity hypothesis it generally does not. For both theories the rate of return on capital, and indeed the ratio of (net) profits to revenue, will vary with the threat of entry, so that in both cases we would expect barrier-to-entry variables to play a role in the determination of profitability so defined. The problem is that despite the masses of results there are none which relate very closely to the degree of monopoly. Most of the studies for the USA, where of course the vast majority of results have been obtained, relate to alternative measures of the rate of return on capital. However, where price—cost margins have been used, the closest approximation to the degree of monopoly has treated overhead labour costs as elements of short-run marginal cost.[38] Clearly barriers-to-entry variables can have a significant, positive impact on such price—cost margin variables while the degree of monopoly remains unaffected. This could happen if higher barriers implied lower levels of excess capacity in response to potential entry. In the case of the UK just about all the results relate to price—cost margins defined in the same way. There is plenty of evidence that barriers to entry do have a positive and significant impact on the rate of return on capital and on price-cost margins, defined as above (for example, see Comanor and Wilson, 1967). However, the barrier variable which turns out to have a consistently major role in the determination of the rate of return on capital, the intensity of advertising, is also likely to be a determinant of the degree of monopoly, so that the interpretation of the advertising result is not unambiguous. As far as concentration is concerned there has been some questioning of the significance of its role in determining the degree of monopoly, but Weiss (1974) concluded from his survey of the world-wide evidence at that time that a significant, positive relationship had been established. This question will be examined more closely in Chapter 5, where the evidence on the link between concentration and the degree of monopoly will form part of the assessment of the link between concentration and wage share. The conclusion we will come to is in accordance with the earlier conclusion drawn by Weiss.

The Degree of Monopoly and the Share of Profits

Our analysis of oligopoly in previous sections identifies the determinants of the mark-up of price on marginal cost within a specific industry. We now have to make plausible assumptions about the typical form of cost—output relationships and about the constituents of variable and overhead costs in the case of short-run price—output decisions by the typical monopolist or oligopolist. It would seem both convenient and realistic to assume constant marginal costs. This is convenient since it allows us to write down the degree of monopoly in a particular industry (μ_k) as the ratio of profits (Π_k^*) plus overhead costs (F_k) to total revenue ($p_k X_k$):

$$\mu_k = \frac{\Pi_k^* + F_k}{p_k X_k}$$

It is realistic, since there is an abundance of statistical evidence that modern production processes are characterised by constant operating costs up to near capacity working (see, for example, Johnston, 1960), and it will be our working assumption that monopoly capital works with some degree of excess capacity, planned or unplanned. In addition to the reasons for excess capacity advanced to this point, which relate to the implications of actual or potential rivalry within the oligopoly world, we also have the Chenery (1952) result, that in a world of monopoly or oligopoly, with economies of scale and growing demand, excess capacity represents an optimal strategy, without taking account of its contribution as a weapon in oligopolistic rivalry.[39] Under the conditions assumed, and with plausible assumptions about the size of scale economies, the rate of discount and the planning period, the normal expectation would be that plants would be built consistent with demands a number of years ahead.[40] The existence of planned excess capacity as a normal case in a world in which firms possess some degree of monopoly power does, of course, following our earlier analysis, allow such positions of market power to be sustained or enhanced. The normal existence of excess capacity will render the coexistence of rivalry and collusion the general case. In addition these micro foundations for planned levels of excess capacity can be supplemented by the general expectation that monopoly capitalism will tend to throw up long periods of capacity underutilisation due to underlying and fundamental contradictions.[41] We therefore have a pretty solid basis for assuming that constant marginal costs will normally prevail. If we now assume that marginal costs comprise the wage costs of operatives and material costs, then F_k includes interest, rent, depreciation and salaries, on the reasonable assumption that the salariat is synonymous with overhead labour.[42] π_k^* is the maximum level of profit in the kth industry, given the values of H_k, α_k and η_k. The existence of managerialism can imply that reported profits are actually less than π_k^*, in which case they will appear in an inflated value of F_k, for example as higher managerial salaries (for detailed discussion see Chapters 3 and 4).

Following from our definition of μ_k, profits plus overheads are equal to the product of sales revenue and the degree of monopoly:

$$p_k \, X_k \, \mu_k = \Pi_k^* + F_k$$

If we now sum over $1, \ldots, N$ industries and divide through by aggregate turnover $(T = \Sigma_k \, p_k \, X_k)$, then we derive the result that the weighted average degree of monopoly $(\bar{\mu})$ is equal to the ratio of gross capitalist income plus salaries $(\Pi * + F)$ to aggregate turnover (T),

$$\frac{\sum\limits_{k} p_k \, X_k \, \mu_k}{\sum\limits_{k} p_k \, X_k} = \bar{\mu} = \frac{\Pi * + F}{T}$$

Although this result refers to a specific short-run situation, it will carry over to the long run if for each vintage of capital the assumption of constant marginal operating costs is preserved, since, although costs may fall, the degree of monopoly is still the sole determinant of $(\Pi* + F)/T$. The degree of monopoly may of course be determined by technology, but the effect on distribution comes only indirectly, that is via the level of concentration, the degree of collusion or the elasticity of demand. Baran and Sweezy (1966) are not very clear on this point: they argue that profit margins will increase as capitalists cut costs, without being very precise about what is happening to the degree of monopoly, so we will digress for a while to consider their theory before going on to derive the implications of the degree of monopoly for the distributive shares.

Surplus in the Baran and Sweezy model comprises profits, interest payments, rent, unproductive expenses and waste, defined as potential output minus actual output. Their concept therefore includes actual and unrealised surplus, and their law of rising surplus states that surplus will tend to rise over time as monopolists/oligopolists strive to cut production worker and material costs. To get this result they assert that 'declining costs imply continuously widening profit margins' and 'provisionally equate aggregate profits with society's economic surplus' (see Baran and Sweezy, 1966, p. 80). Whilst their notion of surplus raises a number of familiar problems, we want to concentrate here on the prediction of an increasing degree of monopoly due to a continuously downward-shifting marginal cost curve. The implicit assumption is that the equilibrium price is invariant to the level of marginal cost, at least in a downward direction.[43] Thus they are going back to Sweezy's earlier notion of the kinked oligopoly demand curve (see Sweezy, 1939). Their asymmetric treatment of price adjustment to changes in marginal cost, with prices rigid if marginal cost is rising,[44] inevitably implies that the degree of monopoly can only increase or remain constant over time. In terms of our model their analysis implies a link between the reduction in marginal cost, coming about via capital accumulation and/or technical change, and a fall in the elasticity of demand, and/or a rise in the degree of collusion and/or the level of concentration. These are clearly possibilities which need spelling out.

A reduction in the price elasticity of demand with a fall in marginal cost could come about, for example, in the case of linear demand. Thus industries with relatively rapid rates of technical progress would be moving more rapidly to inelastic portions of their respective demand curves and would therefore experience relative increases in their degree of monopoly (μ_k). This would provide a link between changes in profit share and the rate of technological progress as measured across different industries. But as productivity increases, so aggregate income will increase and the demand curves facing specific industries will tend to shift out. If they retain the same slope, then the effect we have just isolated will tend to be amplified. At a given initial equilibrium price p^*, the elasticity of demand will have decreased; thus, given H, α and marginal cost, p^* has to rise and therefore the degree of monopoly must also increase. In a recession the reverse will be true. A shift to the left will imply an increase in the elasticity of demand at p^* and therefore p^* must fall and likewise μ.

Turning now to the implications of falling marginal cost for the degree of collusion (α), the kinked demand curve hypothesis would predict an increase in α. Thus price will not be cut, or output will not be increased, because of the feared response of rivals. This hypothesis will be sustained by the general availability of excess capacity which makes the feared response credible. At the limit each firm would expect to move along a demand curve with a slope equal to the industry demand curve for a price cut, since each firm would assume that the proportional cut in prices would be imitated by all rivals, which is equivalent to assuming $\alpha = 1$. The response is not to cut price. The presumed intense rivalry sustains price in the face of cuts in marginal cost.[45] We can therefore reinterpret Sweezy in terms of our model and we see it is supportive of our previous general conclusion on the coexistence of rivalry and collusion. The kinked demand curve is simply a special case.[46]

Lastly the level of concentration may rise as technological innovations are made which are aimed at cutting wage labour costs. This is likely to happen if such innovations imply increased scale economies, and as we have argued earlier, this is very plausible. This puts technology in its rightful secondary role in questions of distribution. It can only work via the degree of monopoly, but it will in turn be chosen for this role, as well as for reasons of efficiency. This contrasts with neo-classical theory, where technology has a central role in distribution theory. Distribution is determined by the elasticity of substitution in production, which is determined exogenously and is embedded in the prevailing technology.

We have seen above that there are situations where the predictions of Baran and Sweezy concerning the growth of the degree of monopoly following reductions in marginal cost will be borne out, and indeed it would appear descriptive of what actually happened in the 1930s.[47] At first sight it would appear to have little relevance in the present world economic situation with high rates of cost and price inflation. Under these conditions industries with falling marginal costs and rigid prices are going to be rather rare. However, perhaps the Sweezy kinked demand curve hypothesis needs reinterpreting in terms of the growth rates of prices and costs. Thus an inflationary world may result in a lack of flexibility about growth rates of prices, so that any tendency for the growth rate of costs to fall would not necessarily bring about a similar reduction in growth rate of prices, each participant in the oligopoly group fearing that this would be seen as an aggressive act by rivals, so that the degree of monopoly would tend to rise. However, whilst this may seem a plausible explanation of what might happen in cyclical down-turns, or in specific industries with rapid rates of growth in productivity, the hypothesis would seem no longer to possess the generality it may have had in the Great Depression. Certainly it should not be seen as explaining any secular tendency.

We can now return to the link between the degree of monopoly and the share of profits. If we multiply through by the ratio of aggregate turnover (T) to Gross National Income (Y), and if we assume all domestic industries are vertically integrated,[48] then $Y = T - M$, where M = expenditure on imports, and we get the share of Gross Capitalist Income plus salaries in Gross National Income to be linearly related to the ratio of expenditure on imports to Gross National Income, with the intercept and slope of the relationship being the degree of monopoly:[49]

$$\frac{\Pi^* + F}{Y} = \bar{\mu} \left(1 + \frac{M}{Y}\right) \tag{2.5}$$

Thus, for a given technology,[50] profit share will increase as (i) the degree of monopoly increases, and (ii) the price of imported materials increases, where aggregate output and its composition are given.[51] Thus we have the perhaps plausible result that increases in market concentration, advertising and collusive practices, working via the degree of monopoly, will tend to raise the profit share, but also the superficially less plausible result that as the import share rises, so does the share of profits. This conclusion deserves close inspection and will be considered in detail in Chapter 6. For the time being, we can say that, so long as imports are processed through the domestic mark-up mechanism captured by $\bar{\mu}$, then this result will indeed hold. The easiest example of this to envisage would be where M is simply expenditure on imported raw materials which then enter the domestic (monopolised) manufacturing sector and are marked up to satisfy the profit-maximising equilibrium described by equation 2.1. The same sort of argument can be made in the case of imports which are intermediate goods (e.g. car components) or final consumer goods (e.g. cars), so long as they are marketed via the domestic (monopolised) retailing sector, again captured within the parameter $\bar{\mu}$. Thus the substitution of Cologne Ford cars for Dagenham Ford cars by the Ford retailing network within the UK will in itself tend to raise the share of profits within the UK economy, i.e. part of the wage share in Ford cars will have been shifted from UK workers to German workers. Tape recorders with a Thorn Electric label, but with a 'Made in Korea' stamp on the back, would represent the same phenomenon. In either case the domestic degree of monopoly would be unimpaired, or even enhanced (see Chapter 6), as the share of imports rose, leaving profit share within the domestic economy higher as a result.[52] This, of course, is not the only possibility. Imports can result in higher levels of excess capacity in domestic industry, implying that the share of overhead costs increase, thereby squeezing the share of net profits, and, of course, they may lower the aggregate degree of monopoly by being directly competitive with domestic industry. Whether this turns out to be the case or not depends on the extent to which domestic monopolies or oligopolies control imports into the system, or are part of some trans-national organisation within which control is vested.[53]

Two further qualifications are necessary. First our aggregation procedures have ignored interdependencies across industries when clearly the degree of monopoly in any one industry may be conditional on that in other industries. It would be possible to determine the general equilibrium set of prices in the economy, but it would be complicated, and, since the relevant matrix of inter-industry coefficients would be essentially unknown, it would not seem particularly useful to pursue. The other issue is that of the determination of the degree of monopoly for British exports. Clearly the degree of monopoly in foreign currency will be determined by market structures in the specific foreign markets, but the mark-up in terms of the domestic currency, e.g. sterling, will also be affected by the exchange rate.[54]

Appendix: Derivation of the Link between Market Structure and the Degree of Monopoly

We assume there are n firms producing and selling a homogeneous product in the kth industry. Each firm will have a profit function.

$$\Pi_{ik}^* = p_k X_{ik} - c_{ik}(X_{ik}) - F_{ik} \qquad i = 1, 2, \ldots n \quad (A2.1)$$

where X_{ik} is the ith firm's output $(\Sigma_i X_{ik} = X_k)$, p_k is the market price, $c_{ik}(X_{ik})$ defines the ith firm's variable cost function and F_{ik} its level of fixed costs. The first-order condition for profit maximisation is

$$\frac{d\Pi_{ik}^*}{dX_{ik}} = p_k + X_{ik} \frac{dp_k}{dX_k} \frac{dX_k}{dX_{ik}} - c_{ik}'(X_{ik}) = 0 \qquad (A2.2)$$

Multiplying by X_{ik} and summing over the n firms yields the industry equilibrium:[55]

$$\frac{\Sigma_i p_k X_{ik} - \Sigma_i X_{ik} c_{ik}'(X_{ik})}{p_k X_k} = \frac{H_k}{\eta_k}(1 + \lambda_k) \qquad (A2.3)$$

where:[56]

$$H_k = \Sigma_i \left\{ \frac{X_{ik}}{X_k} \right\}^2 , \quad \eta_k = \frac{d \log X_k}{d \log p_k} \text{ and } \lambda_k = \frac{\Sigma_i \lambda_{ik} X_{ik}}{\Sigma_i K_{ik}^2}$$

with

$$\lambda_{ik} = \frac{d \Sigma_{j \neq i} X_{jk}}{dX_{ik}}$$

Thus the degree of monopoly will be directly related to the Herfindahl measure of concentration (H) and inversely related to the absolute value of the industry price elasticity of demand (η). The degree of monopoly will also be determined by λ, which captures the firm's expectations concerning the response by rivals to its own output decisions. These expectations could be different for each firm so λ is interpreted as a weighted average of such expectations. Because the magnitude of λ is partly determined by the number of rivals,[57] it is more useful for our purposes to rewrite equation (A2.3), in the form

$$\frac{p_k - c_k'(X_k)}{p_k} = \frac{\alpha_k}{\eta_k} + \frac{(1-\alpha_k)H_k}{\eta_k} \qquad (A2.4)$$

where

$$\alpha_k = \frac{dX_{jk}}{dX_{ik}} \cdot \frac{X_{ik}}{X_{jk}}$$

strictly constant for all i, j, but it could be loosely interpreted as the average response by rivals.

Notes to Chapter 2

1. Materials costs will also comprise part of marginal cost but will come out in the aggregate wash for the closed economy. For the open economy the share of profits plus overheads will also be determined by the share of imports.
2. It should be made clear straightaway that various critiques (e.g. Johnson, 1973; Ferguson, 1969; Kaldor, 1955) have undoubtedly made too much of this. Kalecki did describe the changes in market structure he felt would bring about changes in his measure of the degree of monopoly. Nevertheless it was the case that he did not *derive* any link between market structure and the degree of monopoly, and so it seems worthwhile to outline such a derivation in order to secure more effectively our theoretical perspective on income distribution. It will also supply us with a clearer idea about how capitalists can act to shift the distribution of income in their favour.
3. Empirical evidence on market structure will be reviewed in Chapter 4.
4. It is a simple matter to demonstrate the stability of the Cournot equilibrium from below; see, for example, Nicholson (1972).
5. We have chosen to assume that quantity and not price is the decision variable. In the case of homogeneous product industries this must be the case, as only one price will normally exist. In the case of heterogeneous product industries there are still grounds for assuming that quantity competition will dominate price competition, either because of the instability provoked by price competition in the case of slightly differentiated products where the cross-elasticities between firms within the same industry are high (see Waterson, 1976), or because of uncertainty about marginal costs in the region of profit-maximising output (see Weitzman, 1974).

6. It should be noted that where marginal cost functions vary across firms collusion may imply that the output of one or more firms goes to zero, which is inconsistent with the notion of a constant α across the firms. In the symmetric case (equal market shares) this inconsistency does not arise, and in the non-symmetric case with product heterogeneity it is going to be less important.

7. There are obviously many theories of oligopoly but they simply relate to the value of α. Of course some assume α will be different for output increases (price cuts) compared with output reductions (price increases). Such kinked demand curve theories are discussed later in this chapter when we examine some predictions of Baran and Sweezy.

8. For example, *Electrical Equipment for Mechanically Propelled Land Vehicles* (1963) *Cellulosic Fibres* (1968), *Electric Lamps* (1968), *Starch, Glucoses and Modified Starches* (1971), *Chloriazepoxide and Diazepam* (1973) and *Plasterboard* (1973). Many reports of the Price Commission reveal the same sort of behaviour (see Hazledine, 1979).

9. In addition some mark-ups have changed dramatically over time in ways which are in line with profit-maximising predictions (see Holton, 1957).

10. This point will be taken up later. We are simply saying that wants or tastes are not purely exogeneous — they are malleable, and the advertising activities of corporations will be directed towards moving tastes in the right direction, as seen by the corporation.

11. Marglin (1974) has argued convincingly that the factory system itself was innovated for distributional reasons rather than for reasons of efficiency. We are simply extending the argument from control in the labour market, and over the labour process, to control over the product market. Firms will become bigger for reasons of market dominance, as well as for reasons of efficiency, and technologies suited to large-scale organisations will therefore be encouraged.

12. Stigler's model treats price as the decision variable, but the same idea could be easily translated to the case of quantity competition.

13. Stigler in fact isolates the Herfindahl index as the appropriate measure of concentration. He also identifies the probability of repeat purchasing and the level of concentration among buyers as determinants of the degree of collusion. Higher probabilities of repeat purchasing and lower levels of buyer concentration tend to promote effective collusion among sellers and therefore tend to raise the degree of monopoly.

14. Our model, and our discussion to this point, has referred to collusion over output—price policies, but the same arguments would apply to advertising and product quality policies. It is often suggested that the retaliatory lag will be extended in the case of such competitive strategies, in which case we would observe a higher degree of collusion over output—price policies than for

advertising and product quality policies. In so far as this implies *higher* levels of expenditure on advertising and product differentiation activities, then entry into such a market is made more difficult, an issue which is taken up later. However, the general result is that the degree of monopoly will not be reduced by such competitive activities, and may even be enhanced, but the resultant additional overhead costs will eat into profits so that we may get monopoly pricing without the full appearance of monopoly profits.

15. We mentioned earlier Stigler's results, which indicated a role for the probability of repeat purchasing and the level of concentration among buyers. Both factors are potentially malleable by sellers who seek to dominate the market.

16. The advertising of cigarettes is an interesting case in point. By encouraging the young to begin to smoke via a suitable bombardment of advertising messages, the tobacco monopolies can begin the process whereby addiction is created and consumers (smokers) become very insensitive to increases in price. Some econometric work by McGuiness and Cowling (1975) has demonstrated that total expenditure on the advertising of cigarettes does influence total expenditure on cigarettes and is not simply frittered away in inter-brand competition as the tobacco industry has argued.

17. The paper by Boyer (1974) demonstrates a sharp distinction between the impact of advertising in the case of manufacturing industry and in the case of distributive industries. In the latter case advertising appeared negatively related to price—cost margins, whereas in the case of manufacturing there was a positive relationship. This does not rule out the possibility that the *total* effect of advertising in the distribution sector is not to raise price—cost margins, as Boyer's relationships also included market structural variables.

18. Only firm size appears insignificant. This may reflect the fairly widely reported result that the relationship between the rate of return on capital and firm size is often negative for the UK and Europe in general. The dependent variable is quite close to a measure of profit, given that important elements of overhead costs have been deducted from value-added.

19. Some may interpret this result in terms of advertising as a barrier to entry. We will argue later that the degree of monopoly is invariant to the conditions of entry into the market and therefore we would regard this interpretation of the result as invalid.

20. The other exception to this general antipathy is where an evenly balanced oligopoly group has got into a position of competitive advertising where profits are being seriously threatened. Such was the case in the US cigarette industry at the time a restriction of advertising on health grounds was being mooted by the government. The industry welcomed the regulation, it was enacted and profits dramatically improved. In contrast, in the case of the UK the industry was dominated by one firm (Imperial Tobacco),

advertising intensity was lower and closer to the monopoly level, and any external restriction would have pulled it down below the optimal level as seen by the industry. The industry therefore vigorously resisted any attempt to regulate cigarette advertising and has continued to do so to the present day.

21. There is a problem of interpretation here. Do consumers become more habitual in their behaviour over time simply as a result of their greater average income and wealth, or are they encouraged to become more habitual, in the sense of becoming less sensitive to higher prices, by the rising secular wave of advertising? Since Houthakker and Taylor did not include advertising in their empirical work it is not possible to say. The same is unfortunately the case with most demand analysis working at the market, as opposed to the firm, level. Some studies of demand for specific commodities have included advertising, but no attempt has been made to examine the interrelationship with the price elasticity of demand, although the results reported earlier on advertising and the degree of monopoly provides indirect evidence.

22. A more detailed analysis of potential entry in the context of inter-national trade and investment will be developed in Chapter 6.

23. This led Stigler to the remark that the oligopoly problem was being solved by murder: that is, the question of the interaction among firms in the market is put on one side and the focus is entirely on potential, rather than actual, rivalry. Stigler implied that entry conditions are not sufficient to determine the degree of monopoly.

24. We are taking the (rather restrictive) Stigler view here, that economies of scale are not classified as a barrier to entry.

25. This possible approach had been alluded to previously (see, for example, Modigliani, 1958).

26. Implicit in this argument is the assumption of a basic asymmetry between the existing group and the entrant in the expected post-entry equilibrium. This would seem reasonable given that the group is already there and has committed itself to a strategy which cannot be immediately reversed should entry occur. Thus we would expect post-entry Stackleberg equilibrium rather than a more symmetric view of interdependence.

27. Modigliani's result needs reiterating here. Since high mark-ups tend to be associated with low price elasticities of demand, any increase in output following entry will have a significant depressive impact on price, and the proportional increase in output will be conditioned by scale economies and the size of the market.

28. We are assuming here that the expected price post-entry, which is determined by the availability of capacity and the willingness to use it, is the only thing of interest to the prospective entrant. Price pre-entry, being highly flexible, provides no additional credibility to the threatened price post-entry and will therefore not be lowered to some so-called 'limit price'.

29. This focuses attention on the capital-goods characteristics of

advertising as providing the barrier to potential entrants (see Cowling, 1976).

30. The possibility of excess capacity in distribution, and more broadly in non-internationally tradeable goods, may provide an interesting source of observations on this hypothesis. Whilst in the case of internationally tradeable goods the excess capacity may be actually used for exports, in the case of non-tradeable goods this will not prove possible. This implies that planned excess capacity, as a response to entry, will be more readily observable in this sector. Excessive numbers of check-out points at supermarkets, banks and building societies may be relatively trivial examples; excessive numbers of banks, building societies and petrol filling stations may be less trivial cases, as may be office blocks which stand unlet for many years. The Centre Point phenomenon is very difficult to explain otherwise, since profits can always be raised with short-term leases at low rents. A huge block lying idle for more than ten years must signify some degree of monopoly control in the speculative office building industry, as well as an attempt to retain such control by offering the credible threat of flooding the market with new office space should anyone attempt to enter.

31. See Select Committee on Science and Technology (1971, particularly p. 249).

32. Some would take the argument a stage further and suggest that, given the monopolist or existing oligopoly group can be expected to have the capability of increasing capacity at least as fast as potential rivals, the threat of an increase in capacity will be sufficient to deter entry (see Hazledine, 1979). Whilst this is clearly a possibility, the pre-emptive commitment to excess capacity does add to the credibility of the threat to raise output should entry take place. An interesting example of an extension of capacity coming after a decision on entry had been made, but before it had actually taken place, is provided by the case of the *Coventry Evening Telegraph* vs the *Coventry Journal*. The *Telegraph* was the established monopoly, the *Journal* was the new entrant. After the *Journal's* announcement of its intention to begin publishing a weekly newspaper in Coventry, the *Telegraph*, an evening newspaper, started producing a weekly newspaper which was actually a free-sheet, with advertising revenue providing its sole income. It was already producing a similar free-sheet in neighbouring towns (e.g. Leamington and Kenilworth), but not in Coventry. The *Coventry Journal* did not survive, and following its demise the Coventry free-sheet was withdrawn and its production centre closed down.

33. As noted earlier, excess capacity could be multi-dimensional, comprising unutilised plant and equipment, underutilised overhead labour (managerial, technical, scientific), unutilised inventions, etc.

34. Again, as mentioned earlier, we are taking an asymmetric view of existing firm or firms and new entrant. If potential entrants believed

that the post-entry oligopoly game were to be played according to Cournot-Nash type rules then investment in excess capacity would not be justified (see Dixit, 1980). But it is precisely the pre-emptive commitment to excess capacity that helps to sustain an asymmetric view of the post-entry game.

35. Interestingly, free trade reduces the cost of holding excess capacity to maintain monopoly positions by allowing surplus capacity to be converted into exports. Thus moves to free trade can help to preserve monopolies in domestic markets (see Blattner, 1972). Extending this analysis, and recognising that potential entrants will typically be other monopolies allows us to see that excess capacity gives the capability of retaliation not only in the same market but also in the markets of potential rivals. Courtaulds is an interesting case in point. With the advent of EFTA, fibre users in the UK claimed that reductions in EFTA duties had not brought about the expected competition among fibre producers. Overseas producers claimed that fear of retaliation by Courtaulds, in their own home markets or in other export markets of importance to them, prevented them undercutting Courtaulds in the UK. Again we have the coexistence of collusion and rivalry, with excess capacity giving a credible basis for fears of retaliation. The evidence is documented in Monopolies Commission (1968, p. 123). As we have observed earlier, small-scale entry can be digested fairly easily. It is common practice on the part of large corporations to allow small, and often new, firms to innovate with new products and then take them over (see for example, Quinn, 1953).

36. Interlocking directorships often involving financial institutions would provide an institutional arrangement for minimising the costs of rivalry.

37. Note that the Herfindahl measure of concentration is bounded within the range zero to one.

38. The typical price–cost margin variable used has been the ratio of value added minus wage and *salary* bill to sales revenue. In some cases capital costs have also been deducted.

39. Scale economies are of course quite consistent with constant marginal costs. We are simply assuming that larger plants have bigger overheads and lower operating costs than smaller plants.

40. This would of course not be true if demand were falling, but this is a rare event. Rising demand is of course quite consistent with rising unemployment.

41. These will be explained in some detail in the next chapter.

42. F_k will also include advertising and marketing expenses and rates. We will make the simple but reasonable assumption that advertising and marketing expenses can be broken down into the other elements of overhead costs at the aggregate level.

43. They are more explicit at an earlier point in their book where they do suggest that under oligopoly prices can be expected to be flexible upwards but not downwards (see Baran and Sweezy, 1966, pp. 71–2).

44. For example, they later argue that if unions are successful in raising wages, any increase in costs will be simply marked up, leaving the profit margin unaffected (see Baran and Sweezy, 1966, pp. 85–6).

45. Stigler's objections can be discounted (see Stigler, 1947). His empirical observations of relative price flexibility in oligopolistic and other markets led him to conclude that Sweezy's hypothesis could not be sustained. However, to test for the existence of a kinked demand curve requires a prediction of optimal price change with and without the existence of the kink. He did not do this and therefore we cannot accept his observations as an adequate test of the hypothesis.

46. Interestingly, evidence from the UK car market provides indirect evidence for the existence of a kinked demand curve and indicates that it has forced oligopolists in this industry into higher levels of product competition. Despite the fact that growth of the crude price index for cars has shown no downward flexibility in times of recession, the 'quality' adjusted price index has (see Cowling and Cubbin, 1972). This implies that, in this case, there was a tendency for the degree of monopoly to be preserved during recessions since marginal costs would be raised by the changes in the product (new or revamped models). If such non-price competition was exclusively in terms of advertising then the degree of monopoly would tend to rise, since list price would not fall with falling marginal costs (or the growth rate of list price would not fall with a falling growth rate in marginal cost), and advertising would leave marginal costs unaffected.

47. Marginal costs of industrial production fell, largely because of the sharp reduction in raw material prices. As a result the degree of monopoly could rise without real wages in the industrialised countries falling. The evidence appears consistent with the Baran and Sweezy story (see Kalecki, 1939).

48. This simplification implies that there are not inter-industry transactions in domestic intermediate goods. If this were allowed then we would have to introduce an input—output matrix which would seem to complicate matters without adding much to our insight into the problem.

49. M at the aggregate level is in fact imported materials, since domestic materials would become someone's value-added.

50. Since technology could influence the value of M/Y, e.g. reduce the import content of British output. We are assuming no substitution in the short run between materials and labour.

51. The exogenous variables in M/Y are p_m, the price of imported materials, and w, the wage rate. Output is determined in the degree of monopoly equation and so, for a given technology, will be the level of employment and imports.

52. For vertically integrated enterprises the actual international incidence of profits will be determined by their transfer pricing policies, which will in turn reflect the international incidence of the rate of

profits tax. Thus although UK value-added in the case of Cologne Fords is essentially profit, the transfer price, and thus the import price, may be set sufficiently high so that no profit from these transactions enters Ford's UK accounts. The same problem does not appear where imported goods are bought and sold by domestic retailing monopolies, e.g. German beer by British breweries with tied outlets.

53. These issues are examined in some detail in Chapter 6.

54. It should also be noted that with a freely floating exhange rate imports in aggregate will not normally become more or less competitive with domestic production.

55. Allowing for product differentiation indicates higher profit margins in equilibrium, a result which seems intuitively plausible.

56. This result is secured by Cowling and Waterson (1976), who then adapted it for empirical investigation.

57. For example, if the expected response by each rival is the same then $\lambda_{ik} = (n_k - 1) \, dX_{jk}/dX_{ik}$. Thus the value λ_k in equation (A2.3) is *directly* affected by changes in concentration, even if the expected response by each rival remains unchanged. λ will automatically fall as concentration increases. As explained below, two opposing effects can be expected; λ will fall as H increases through the number of rivals effect, but will tend to rise with H as the degree of collusion increases, i.e. as dX_{jk}/dX_{ik} increases.

3
The Realisation of Profits

In the previous chapter we have argued that increased market concentration will imply the emerging coexistence of rivalry and collusion, which in turn will lead to a higher sustainable degree of monopoly, as measured by the mark-up of price on marginal cost, and thus to an increased profit share. Thus any tendency for a rising level of market concentration over time allows for the potential existence of a rising profit share. Assuming the composition of marginal cost remains unchanged, that is that the ratio of expenditure on materials to expenditure on wages remains unchanged, then whether or not the share of profits actually increases will be dependent on the maintenance of the level and composition of output, or more accurately in a dynamic world, on the maintenance of the degree of excess capacity consistent with the increased degree of monopoly. If actual excess capacity exceeded planned excess capacity following the growth of monopoly or oligopoly, then although $(\Pi^* + F)/Y$ would tend to rise, this would be reflected wholly or partly in an increase in the share of overheads (F/Y), either as overhead costs were spread over a smaller than planned output, or as the degree of excess capacity increased faster than expected despite a constant or increased output. The basic question is whether the level of aggregate demand will be sufficient to allow the potential profits arising from increased monopoly power to be actually realized. Thus we need to examine how effective demand might change as a result of the underlying tendency for income to be redistributed from workers to capitalists.

Let us take first the simplest possible example of a closed economy with no state expenditures. Then Gross National

Income can be defined as the sum of property income (profit, depreciation, rent and interest) and employment income (wages and salaries), and Gross National Product will be the sum of gross investment, capitalist consumption and worker consumption. If workers receive only wages and salaries and capitalists receive only property income, and if workers consume everything they receive, then it is clear that property income will equal gross investment plus capitalist consumption. This led Kalecki to the remark that capitalists earn what they spend and workers spend what they earn.

If we now look at the more general case of an open economy, with state expenditures, and allow workers to save, then Gross National Income is equal to after-tax gross profits,[1] plus after-tax wages and salaries, plus direct and indirect taxes. Gross National Product can then be written as the sum of gross investment, capitalist consumption, worker consumption, government expenditure and the trade balance (exports minus imports). After a little manipulation the level of gross profits after tax (π^1)[2] can be written as the sum of gross investment (I), capitalist consumption (C_c), the trade balance $(E - M)$, and the budget deficit (B) minus workers savings (W_s):

$$\pi^1 = I + C_c + E - M + B - W_s \qquad (3.1)$$

Thus any tendency for profits to rise because of an increase in the degree of monopoly has to be matched by commensurate changes in these aggregate variables. If we initially preclude any adjustments in the foreign trade balance, or by the state, or workers, i.e. $d(E - M) = dB = dW_s = 0$, then any change in profits will be due to a change in investment and/or capitalist consumption. Thus if capitalists instantaneously adjust to the increased flow of profits arising from their rising monopoly power by spending it on either investment or consumption goods then there will be no realisation crisis. Excluding other adjustments, the onset of a realisation crisis must be due to the fact that capitalists' spending is to a substantial degree predetermined, and indeed that expectations regarding the level of future profits, assuming they are realised, are either poorly formed or not acted on. Thus each corporation acquiring monopoly power either does not fully anticipate the consequences in terms of profits, or does not revise its planned level of expenditure in the light of this. The other possibility is that the immediate effect of monopolisation is the appearance of excess capacity, since that would be consistent with the higher degree of monopoly for a stationary demand function, and this will in itself have a restricting effect on the rate of investment, which may appear as a cut-back in plans which have been already formulated. But this does not preclude an increasing diversion of funds to other sectors which are either not experiencing excess capacity (including competitive sectors) or are experiencing monopoly profits in which the firm in question is not participating.

This discussion does raise the question of the precise conditions under which a planned increase in monopoly power, for example via a process of horizontal merger, will in fact lead to the question of the realisation of profits, since individual capitalists will recognise the consequences of monopoly pricing in terms of excess capacity as well as in terms of profits, and will therefore either anticipate a change in investment policy or will continue to invest in the same market consistent with their attempts to secure a credible deterrent to potential rivals. Thus, since the acquisition of monopoly represents a planned process, and since its maintenance requires investment expenditures, the possibility of a realisation crisis is diminished and may be contrasted with other *unplanned* processes that lead to redistributions favouring profits. Nevertheless, there will always be uncertainty about the change in the level of profits, and thus the distinction Kalecki (1971) draws between capitalist expenditure and worker expenditure is an important one: workers receive and spend income week by week, capitalists do not and therefore do not immediately react to changes in the stream of profits. The problem is not one of matching the behaviour of different groups involved in saving and investing, as Keynes would have it, but one of realising *ex ante* profits via the investment or consumption behaviour of capitalists.

The other major qualification that has to be made about monopolisation as a planned process is that, although it may be planned by each individual capitalist or each specific oligopoly group, nevertheless in aggregate it remains an unplanned process. To the extent that the monopolisation of one sector leads to a *planned* cutback in investment, this will undoubtedly lead to an *unplanned* increase in excess capacity in some other sector vertically linked to the monopolising sector. Thus the planned cut-back in, for example, the steel industry, which may have resulted from a move towards profit-maximising price policies, will bring about an unplanned increase in excess capacity in the coal industry, which will in turn feed through, via a cut-back in output and capacity in the coal industry, to other sectors of the economy.[3] Thus in an integrated national and international economy, processes of monopolisation and their related output and capacity cut-backs, which are planned in each sector in each national economy, will inevitably bring about a series of unplanned cut-backs through the system. Despite planning within the dominant giant corporations the system is still unplanned at the aggregate and international levels. Planning has not replaced anarchy in the capitalist system as a whole and therefore major dislocations are likely to occur following planned monopolisation processes. We therefore conclude that the possibility of a realisation crisis is not significantly diminished by the fact that the underlying process, which leads to the underlying tendency for the distribution of income to change, is itself a planned process at the level of the firm or oligopoly group.

Let us assume that the rate of investment is governed by the rate of profit and the cost of capital in the recent past and that this planned rate of investment can be, to some extent, modified in the current period in the light of experience with regard to the utilisation of existing capacity. Although there are arguments about the specification of investment functions, this view would seem to capture the theoretically and empirically important attributes of such functions. Clearly, actual investment expenditures respond with a lag to variations in profitability and capital costs because of the substantial gestation period involved in producing and installing new plant and equipment. It is therefore difficult to raise the level of investment in the short term, but it is possible to reduce it. Thus if the level of demand for output should fall below the expected level, or if the planned level of output is reduced, then capacity utilisation will fall. It will then appear optimal to the individual firm to eliminate such excess capacity by cutting back on new investment or at least delaying it, wherever possible.[4] This would suggest that an increase in the aggregate degree of monopoly, with effects recognised by some capitalists but certainly not by all, will tend to lead to a cut-back in investment plans in the short term. This will tend to happen because the first observed impact is the general emergence of higher levels of excess capacity. Of course, for those who have planned the monopolisation of particular markets the emergence of excess capacity is a necessary consequence, given that the capital stock cannot be immediately adjusted to the reduction in the rate of output, or the reduction of the growth in the rate of output in the case of a growing economy, and they will also anticipate the increase in profits following, after some lag, from their actions. However, even in this case the rate of investment is unlikely to rise immediately because the firm or firms in question have to identify a new area of investment given that their optimal capacity in existing markets has been effectively reduced.[5]

It remains to demonstrate that in fact the level of capacity utilisation does have a significant impact on investment. The empirical record would appear to suggest strongly that this is indeed the case.[6] Chenery (1952) examined investment behaviour in six US industries over the period 1922–39 and found that the capacity formulation of the accelerator model performed much better than the simple accelerator in the case of the four oligopolies with high capital intensities (steel, cement, electricity and zinc), whereas the simple accelerator was slightly better in the two competitive, low-capital-intensity industries (petroleum[7] and paper and paperboard). Also at the industry level, the Motor Manufacturing Economic Development Committee (EDC) (1970) and the Chemicals EDC (1971) both attributed cut-backs in planned investment to the emergence of overcapacity and lower than expected growth in sales. The CBI Investment Intentions Survey, the results for the previous five years being tabulated in Peretz (1976), again clearly reveal the importance of excess capacity. Apart from one survey in 1974, between 71 per cent and 83 per cent of respondents gave 'adequate capacity' as the major factor expected to limit actual investment. At the aggregate level Smyth and Briscoe (1971) found both the level and rate of change of capacity utilisation to be highly significant in explaining the rate of investment for each of the periods 1923–38 and 1950–66. These results are supported by Nobay (1970) and Burman (1970), with Burman claiming that most of the variation in investment in manufacturing was due to variations in capacity utilisation, although less so for new buildings than for machinery. This last point fits our view of the investment process since it will generally be easier to cut back on planned investment in machinery than it would be in the case of new buildings. Panić and Vernon (1975) examined a range of UK manufacturing industries and concluded that most investment took place when demand promised to cause serious and prolonged pressure on capacity. They also concluded, along with the Machine Tool EDC (1973), that the desire to invest in manufacturing in the early 1970s had evaporated due to the high levels of excess capacity then prevailing.

Given this mass of evidence of a strong link between capacity utilisation and the rate of investment, we conclude that the immediate effect of an increase in the aggregate degree of monopoly is to reduce the level of actual investment below its planned level, and this will in turn imply that the level of profit, or its rate of growth, will tend to be depressed. This in turn means that the planned rate of investment will tend to fall back, since in the longer term it will be determined by the rate of profit compared with the cost of capital. This then means that orders to the capital goods sector will be reduced and thus a secondary wave of cut-backs in output and investment will have been initiated.

A simplified formal representation of the argument would be:

$$I_t = F \left\{ \frac{\Pi'}{K} \right\}^{t-\theta} ; i_{t-\theta} ; CU_t ; \dot{CU}_t \qquad (3.2)$$

$$CU_t = g\left(\mu_t\right) \qquad (3.3)$$

where K is capital stock, i is the cost of capital, CU is the rate of capital utilisation and $\dot{CU}$ its rate of change, and μ is the degree of monopoly. $\theta > 0$ is the length of lag in the response of actual investment to profit rate and capital cost.[8] These assumptions imply that $dI_t/d\mu_t < 0$, which in turn implies a downward spiral in profits, investment and therefore output, unless compensating movements in the other elements on the right-hand side of (3.1) result.[9] This is a suitable point at which to consider capitalist consumption.

The classical theory of saving behaviour postulates a propensity to save out of profits which exceeds the propensity to save out of wages, and thus the distribution of income enters as an important determinant of the equilibrium growth-rate of the economy.[10] Ricardo argued that savings were not possible out of wages, because of the requirements of subsistence, while landlords spent their income on luxury consumption. Capitalists saved a considerable portion of their income because they associated their power with their ownership of capital. Marxian analysis has stressed the necessity of accumulation for survival. Thus capitalist rivalry meant that unless an individual capitalist were able to expand his scale of operations at the same rate as that of others, his profits would fall relatively, and therefore so too would his rate of accumulation. Such a cumulative process would ensure the inevitable but premature demise of such a capitalist.

Under competitive capitalism it may be reasonable to assume the Marxian imperative to accumulate in order to survive, but in a world of monopoly or oligopoly this condition must be severely qualified. Investment to maintain the monopoly from encroachment could be the new imperative, but the option is always there to accept the competitive rate of return.[11] Thus in a private, individual sense monopoly removes the requirement of accumulation and growth, but in a global sense the requirement of accumulation to realise profits is maintained or enhanced, given a tendency for monopolisation to increase. In the same global sense accumulation will be required in the longer term to sustain the system itself. Capitalism survives because it delivers the goods, but given rising expectations, this implies that a positive growth rate in real wages is maintained, and this in turn requires positive net investment. Thus accumulation is the key to social stability in both the short and long term. Capitalist consumption could however fill the gap in the short term, while raising problems in the longer term. Thus, if in a monopolising economy the capitalist class were increasingly to adopt the habits and lifestyle of the landed aristocracy, then this could provide a solution to the latent realisation crisis. Income would be shifting from workers with a high propensity to consume to capitalists with an initially lower but rising propensity to consume. The very profligacy of the capitalist class could postpone an immediate crisis, but by holding back accumulation could eventually precipitate a deeper one. In underdeveloped countries Baran (1957) has emphasised that the bourgeoisie have sought to imitate the cultural habits of the socially dominant group, the landed aristocracy, and this has favoured conspicuous consumption rather than accumulation. Under monopoly capitalism this would seem a more general phenomenon, particularly where the bourgeois revolution has been incomplete so that the pre-capitalist ruling class retains some degree of cultural dominance,[12] but it may also represent an adaptation over time to increasing wealth. Papanek's observations on the behaviour of industrial capitalists in Pakistan make an interesting case. During the 1950s the newly formed industrial bourgeoisie revealed high rates of saving, 'their wants increased much more slowly than their income', whereas by the 1960s their consumption expenditures seemed to be catching up with their income (Papanek, 1967).

The existence of a world of managerial capitalism has two implications for this process. First, managers faced with a capitalist class anxious to consume will prefer to retain profits rather than distribute them; and second, as well as preferring retentions to the distribution of profits, they also will prefer consumption — their own consumption — to the generation of profits, at least up to a point. On retained earnings, Lambrinides (1973) argues that it is the retentions policies of corporations which sustain the classical saving function, implying that a shift from wages to profits will raise aggregate savings only with the intervention of the corporation and despite the savings behaviour of capitalists. This view has also been put forward by Marglin (1974), who argues that households spend everything they can lay their hands on, with saving only occurring when incomes are rising faster than the rate at which spending behaviour can be adjusted. Only the interposing of hierarchical control prevents society from ending the process of accumulation.[13] This is an extreme view which implies that redistributions between wages and profits will have no effect on the aggregate propensity to save unless it is coupled with higher retentions by the corporate sector. In this view of contemporary capitalism corporations are there to save by withholding income from the owners, or at least some of the owners, of capital,[14] and households are there to consume, and they are instructed to do so by the corporations. Whilst the thrust of this argument is convincing, it would seem to be flying in the face of empirical evidence to suggest that the equilibrium propensity to save out of property income will be the same as out of wage income. It would seem more accurate to suggest that an increase in corporate saving can be expected to raise the aggregate rate of saving, but that a shift from wages to profits will also achieve this, even in the absence of an increase in retentions. We may expect a higher propensity to save out of profits than out of wages because it represents an income with higher variance and because it accrues to the richer elements of society, although there is no totally compelling theory to sustain the latter argument.

Recent empirical evidence on this issue is rather limited since most contemporary work on the consumption function neglects the possible impact of changes in the functional distribution of income, and indeed changes in the share of corporate income and saving. Kalecki (1971a) examined the period 1929–40 in the USA and estimated the marginal propensity to consume out of gross capitalist income to be 0.25, assuming that the propensity to save out of wages and salaries were zero.[15] Since retained earnings are not separately identified, this result, although suggestive, cannot refute the Marglin hypothesis. However, the work of Klein and Goldberger (1955) and Klein *et al.* (1961) offers more direct evidence for the USA and the UK. They estimate a Koyck version of the aggregate consumption function and include two income variables, after-tax wage income and after-tax non-wage personal income (i.e. dividends, rent and interest), and in the case of the UK report long-run, base-year elasticities of 0.44 and 0.13 respectively. Burmeister and Taubman (1969) split US income into labour incomes, rent and interest on the one hand, and dividends and self-employment income on the other, on the grounds that this split maximises the significance of the difference in savings propensities. This probably indicates that it is the variability of the income which explains the difference in savings propensities. More recently an unpublished study by Murfin (1980) lends considerable support to the Klein *et al.* finding that the marginal propensity to consume for workers is more than three times that for capitalists. Thus the limited evidence would suggest Marglin's position is too extreme.[16]

But what about the importance of corporate retentions in maintaining or increasing the aggregate savings ratio? Lambrinides (1974) estimates an aggregate savings equation along Ando-Modigliani lines, but dividing income into personal income (Y_p) and corporate saving Π_R. The neo-classical hypothesis would imply that the parameter on Y_p would be the same as the parameter on Π_R because both corporate saving and personal saving are under the control of individuals and thus the coefficients on the two variables should not be significantly different from each other. The alternative, managerial theory, is that corporations will tend to save more than individuals would freely choose to do, and thus the coefficient on Π_R should be significantly bigger than the coefficient on Y_p.[17] Using annual data for the period 1919–58 the coefficients on Y_p and Π_R were each well determined with the coefficient on Π_R being at least double that on Y_p.[18] A reallocation of ten million dollars of capitalist income from individuals to corporations would apparently increase saving by between two and four million dollars.

The above empirical evidence points to the conclusion that a redistribution from wages to profits will have a depressive impact on consumption and this will be maximised where the increment of profit is retained within the corporation rather than being distributed to stockholders.[19] But this is not the whole managerial story. As well as preferring retentions to the distribution of profits, managers will also prefer to raise some forms of expenditure within the corporation at the expense of reported profits. Thus although on the surface a shift from wages to profits will appear to lead to a higher level of savings, part of the underlying shift will tend to be disguised by the absorption of profits within the managerial hierarchy in the form of pecuniary and non-pecuniary income.

Managerialism is usually portrayed in terms of a conflict between managers and stockholders reflecting a dichotomy between ownership and control. In this chapter and the next we will seek to identify two basic struggles involving managers and stockholders, one between big capital and small capital, with big capital occupying a normally dominant position *within* the corporation, and the other between high-level and lower-level management, where high-level management includes the important representatives of big capital. In discussing retentions we have been focusing on one aspect of the struggle between big capital and small capital, with big capital enforcing a dividend policy which will not normally fully reflect the preferences of other fractions of capital. In this interpretation managers at the top level who are taking such decisions are required to make a sacrifice since they are themselves major shareholders; but such abstinence is more apparent than real. The greater investment made will contribute directly to their own power, status and prestige and will provide the seed corn for their own future internal consumption activities. It is to these activities to which we now turn. They represent a further facet of the struggle between management and the external owners of the corporation, who are not participants in such intra-corporation consumption of profits.

Oliver Williamson's (1964) analysis of managerialism provides an appropriate framework for our discussion at this point. He sought to specify a managerial utility function which captured the essence of what behaviourists had to say about managerial motivation, but in terms of conventional economic categories. Profit entered as one of the arguments of the managerial utility function for a variety of reasons (e.g. as a measure of success and as a source of growth), but various elements of cost also entered as direct determinants of utility, in addition to their contribution to output and therefore profits. Probably the most significant element of cost entering the managerial utility function was staff expenditure. Each level of management would gain utility as more layers were added to the base of the hierarchical pyramid, and of course would gain directly from increases in salary and perquisites at their own level. Staff expenditure would therefore capture the size of the managerial hierarchy and the payments to members of that hierarchy, but other elements of cost would also generate managerial utility directly: the size of office, the quality of furnishings, the 'quality' and number of secretarial staff, executive dining rooms, size of expense account, international conferences, executive aircraft, etc. There is obviously a whole area of expenditure within the corporation which is contributing directly to managerial utility irrespective of its contribution to output. The greater the degree of managerial control, the farther will such expenditures depart from their profit-maximising levels, but the presence of profit in the utility function will provide the ultimate constraint on such activities.

However, while it is safer to assume that managers will follow their own interests wherever possible, rather than behaving as if to maximise the welfare of external holders of stock, it does not follow that they will want to abandon profit-maximising price—output rules implicit in the oligopoly equilibrium we have described in Chapter 2. It seems reasonable to assume that in any short-run situation management will want to maximise the excess of revenue over variable costs, for any given inter-firm arrangement. Having picked the profit-maximising price or output for any degree of collusion which it appears possible to sustain, the problem becomes one of distributing this flow of income between stockholders and management. One aspect of this is to retain more of reported profits than external shareholders would wish, that is, to save and invest more than they would themselves choose to do; the other aspect is to consume part of potential profits within the corporation and hand out part as higher payments to managers. This is reflected in Williamson's model, where the first order condition for short-run profit maximisation is retained. This comes out in the algebra simply because (a) profit is an argument of the utility function, and (b) the cost elements in the determination of short-run output do not enter the utility function and therefore do not push output beyond the profit-maximising level. This is a rather important point because many managerial theories have implied that output will be pushed beyond the profit-maximising point as firms adopt sales-revenue or growth-maximising policies (Baumol, 1967; Marris, 1964). The assumption of sales-revenue maximisation by managerial firms would seem to have little to commend it and seems to be based on anecdotal evidence, whilst growth maximisation would seem to be best approached via the retentions policies of firms. Any price–output policy which represents a departure from profit-maximising behaviour must represent a diversion from growth-maximising policies since, directly or indirectly, this will tend to reduce the firm's access to new capital. To say that current price, advertising and 'product' policies are set with an eye to future as well as present sales is, of course, quite consistent with profit-maximising behaviour. However, the actual level of price can be affected by managerialism, even when we take the more plausible Williamson view of the world. He has argued that the number of staff, and therefore the number of layers in the hierarchy, given a more or less fixed span of control, would enter the managerial utility function. He also assumes that part of these extra staff would represent increased selling effort, and we would expect this to lower the elasticity of demand facing the managerial firm and thus increase the degree of monopoly.[20]

We therefore conclude that managerialism, rather than tending to pull down the share of profits directly by picking output rates in excess of profit-maximising levels, will tend if anything to push up the share of profits by choosing higher levels of overhead labour, some of whom will be involved in the sales effort. This does not of course mean that the higher share of what should be called profits will actually appear as such. Although $(\pi^* + F)/Y$ may rise as a result of managerialism, some expenses like staff expenses, broadly defined, will have been taken beyond the profit-maximising level, and will therefore be eating into π^*. If we regard the effect of managerialism on the degree of monopoly as insignificant then $(\pi^* + F)/Y$ will remain constant, but F/Y will rise and reported profits (π) will be less than π^*, which is now to be interpreted as the upper bound on the level of profits actually reported. The share of reported profits, for any level of aggregate demand, would then be determined by the degree of monopoly and the degree of managerial control. The gap between π^* and π, what has been called discretionary expenditure (D) by Williamson, is determined by the interaction of the degree of monopoly (μ) and the degree of capital market power possessed by management (θ), each being necessary but not sufficient:

$$D = D\left(\mu; \theta\right) \qquad (3.3)$$

where D_μ, $D_\theta > 0$; $D_{\mu\theta}$, $D_{\theta\mu} > 0$; $D\left(0, \theta\right) = D\left(\mu, 0\right) = 0$. θ comprises at least three elements: (1) the ability of (external) stockholders to achieve the displacement of managers, which is likely to be conditional on the dispersion of share-ownership and the composition of the board; (2) the ability of raiders to achieve control via takeover, which is likely to be determined by the size of the company; and (3) the efficiency of the internal control apparatus, which may be conditional, to a large extent, on the organisational structure of the firm.[21] In addition, government regulation and taxation is likely to encourage discretionary expenditure by penalising high *reported* profits. Since *unreported* profits are not taxed or (typically) regulated, and yet provide utility to management, we can expect considerable expansion when reported profits become more tightly constrained by state action. This in itself may work through via θ by reducing the level of profits required to forestall a management displacment effort.

We can now redefine the share of gross capitalist income and salaries in a managerial world:

$$\pi^* = \pi + D\left(\mu, \theta\right)$$

Therefore

$$\pi^* + F = \pi + D\left(\mu, \theta\right) + F$$

and

$$\frac{\pi^* + F}{Y} = \frac{\pi + F'}{Y}$$

where F' represents overhead costs in a managerial world, $F' > F$. Thus for a given level and composition of output, increasing managerialism implies rising overheads and therefore a falling share of reported profits.

Thus under managerial capitalism an increasing degree of monopoly will imply the replacement of worker consumption partly by corporate saving and partly by managerial consumption. The question of a realisation crisis then devolves into a question of the rate of adjustment of managerial consumption (C_M) and corporate investment to the tendency for the share of wages (as opposed to salaries) to fall. Thus

$$\left[\frac{\partial I}{\partial \mu} + \frac{\partial C_M}{\partial \mu} + \frac{\partial C_W}{\partial \mu} \right] d\mu \lesseqqgtr 0$$

where $C_W = W$.[22] A realisation crisis will be avoided where the above expression is equal to, or greater than, zero, that is, where the decline of worker consumption as the degree of monopoly rises is fully, or more than fully, offset by increases in the rate of investment or managerial consumption.

We have argued earlier that investment will tend to fall as excess capacity appears, while profits are essentially predetermined. Although managerial consumption adds a more ambiguous element we would expect that it would be unlikely to offset the decline in worker consumption and investment because (a) the source of increasing managerial consumption, increasing π^*, will be a matter of substantial uncertainty to managers in general, and it will be difficult to raise salaries until there is real evidence of higher profits, and (b) the marginal propensity to consume of salary recipients within the managerial hierarchy may be expected to be less than for wage earners.[23]

Hitherto our discussion has focused on redefined elements of capitalist investment and consumption, but in an open economy, with a state sector and the possibility of saving by workers, other adjustments may be possible which will allow the realisation of profits within a monopolising world.

We can see from our accounting identity (3.1) that if we were to hold capitalist expenditure, the budget deficit, and savings out of wages and salaries constant, then an increase in export surplus would increase gross profits by an equivalent amount. Whether or not this is a possibility in a monopolising world depends on having the excess capacity to supply the extra exports (or replace imports), and also being able to secure these markets. If exports can be increased the wage bill will be raised, which will lead to increased demand for consumption goods, which will in turn mean higher levels of both profits and wages. A new equilibrium will be established when extra profits are just equal to the extra output of the export sector. But what about the link between export surplus and the degree of monopoly? On the import side it would appear that an increased degree of domestic monopoly would tend to lead to an increase in the import of manufactures, given the higher prices in domestic markets. This would be limited by the degree of control domestic monopolies had over the flow of imports, but if monopolisation led to a wage—price spiral, then even with control the level of imports would tend to rise as domestic monopolies switched their sources of supply to foreign producers.[24] In the longer term it has been argued that the monopolisation of the European economies will allow them to compete effectively with American capital (the Servan-Schreiber argument), which could imply that despite the tendency for the degree of monopoly to rise, prices could be lower than in the more competitive case, and thus imports would be lower than they otherwise might be. The evidence collected on the impact of mergers in the UK, and indeed more generally, would not support this view of the world (see Chapter 4).

What of the export side? Whilst the creation of giant firms may not give an advantage in terms of efficiency, the creation of excess capacity in the process of monopolisation and as a consequence of monopolisation provides a necessary precondition for the dumping of any surplus output in foreign markets, (see Blattner, 1972, and the discussion in Chapter 2 on potential entry). However, to be effective on a general scale subsumes the international dominance of a particular national capital. This is certainly not true of the UK, and although it may have been true of the USA prior to the Vietnam war, the international capitalist scene is now characterised by national rivalry rather than by the unchallenged US hegemony of the earlier post-war period. Thus no one capitalist economy can choose to dump its surplus on the international economy — a more even balance of power will restrict such activity. The Third World, and the continued existence of neo-colonial dependency, still provides a potential way out, but one which is restricted by rising nationalism and the ability of the Third World to pay for the products of the advanced capitalist economies.[25] I would conclude that although we may argue that the search for overseas markets to resolve the crisis of the advanced capitalist economies is linked to the monopoly phase of capitalism, nevertheless this way out is becoming increasingly curtailed. The position is worsened by the emergence of a new powerful international monopoly, OPEC, outside the control of the advanced capitalist economies. As a result the export surpluses of these economies have been reduced due to the rising expenditure on energy imports and the inability, or unwillingness, of the OPEC countries to recycle their receipts, despite the former Shah of Iran's best efforts.

If the balance of evidence suggest that a potential realisation crisis cannot be easily resolved by a rising export surplus,[26] there still remains the possibility of more direct state action via rising state expenditures or tax-cutting policies, but these face both technical and ideological constraints. These comprise (a) fine-tuning problems; (b) a deflationary reaction to inflation; and (c) a lack of commitment to full employment. Thus an appropriate and timely budget deficit may be difficult to engineer. This was undoubtedly a problem in the earlier post-war period, given that there was no in-built tendency to stagnation, so that a delayed response by the state to a temporary recession often meant that the stimulus came at a time when the economy was already recovering and therefore led to an adjustment in the price level rather than in the level of output. This problem of fine tuning is still a problem in a period of stagnation, but is less critical. By not acting earlier a downward spiral may become more difficult to cope with, but with considerable excess capacity a budget deficit becomes that much more powerful a tool for raising aggregate output. However, stagnation may be associated with high rates of inflation, and a rising degree of monopoly will tend to accentuate the condition. This may lead the state to hold back from reflationary policies, reflecting the second constraint we have identified but also leading into the third, the commitment to full employment. Under our assumptions, expanding aggregate demand via increased budget deficits can raise output, employment and profits; but there will be dynamic consequences. Whilst Keynes saw both sides, capital and labour, gaining by using the state to make up any deficiency in aggregate demand, Kalecki saw more clearly the underlying dynamic contradictions. Full-employment policies, by increasing the confidence and power of the working class, would lead to a shift in the balance of power between capital and workers. Whilst within certain historical periods, like the early post-war period, full-employment policies may be congruent with the achievement of maximum profits, beyond a certain point of development capital will seek a reversal of policy to regain its former position *vis-à-vis* labour. We cannot therefore assume that an increase in the budget deficit will be forthcoming in response to an emerging realisation crisis. We return to this issue in the later chapters dealing with class struggle and recent history (Chapters 5 and 7).

Having considered the likely response of investment, capitalist consumption, export surplus and the government's budget deficit to an increase in the aggregate degree of monopoly, we are led to the conclusion that a realisation crisis is a distinct possibility and that although Keynesian policies may postpone the advent of such a crisis, there will be inevitable pressures, from within the capitalist class, to jettison such policies as their internal contradictions are revealed. More generally it is clear that the various adjustments required to maintain effective demand, in the presence of a tendency for the wage share to fall, contain the seeds of further and deeper crisis. Thus if effective demand is to be maintained by an increase in the rate of investment, this has immediate implications for the capital stock and therefore the productive capacity of the economy. Capital accumulation is forced to feed on itself, with rising capital accumulation depending on a rising share of capital accumulation. Thus a crisis can be postponed, but the inevitable crisis is likely to be deeper. The 'new technology' (microelectronics) is an interesting and topical example. This may bring a surge in investment, but it also brings a tendency for the share of wages to fall, since the new processes, *once installed*, require much less labour.[27] This implies that employment can only be sustained by an accelerating rate of investment, but this solution would appear highly unstable.

If foreign investment, with its associated export of capital goods is seen as a solution, then the same eventual 'problem' will reappear. What is to be done with the increased flow of profits which will eventually materialise? Export dumping more generally, to some colonial or neo-colonial dependency, may offer a way out, but to finance its continuation requires imports from those Third World countries to rise or capital outflows to take place, from which a profit flow will be forthcoming and has to be spent. In the case of exports to other advanced capitalist economies we would expect rivalry to generate tacit or overt agreements to restrict dumping. We have already mentioned the inevitable reaction to state intervention to solve realisation crises, but there remains the solution offered by rising managerial consumption. Why should not the insatiable desires of managers to raise their own status, power and prestige resolve any latent crisis posed by the monopolisation of the economy? We have already mentioned that there may be a primary problem posed by the less than immediate adjustment of managers to an increased profit flow, but what of the longer term? With the state initially acting to maintain full employment in the face of a monopolisation tendency, can rising managerialism take over the state's role as regulator of effective demand as and when the state bows out under pressure from capital? Although this could appear as a solution it will not be one that can be fully sustained, because rising managerialism, or at least an aspect of it, is seen as a threat not only by the external owners of the firm but also by higher-level management, who will themselves usually have a major interest in the firm. Although managerialism may be seen as an antidote to capitalist crisis at the aggregate level, it will always appear as something to be minimised by those with an interest in the flow of reported profits. The individual or group response of capital interests will therefore be to adopt control systems to minimise descretionary behaviour. We can therefore envisage that managerialism, in the sense of the rising power and discretionary expenditures of those within the managerial hierarchy, rather than at its apex, will generate a reaction which will tend to force corporations back towards profit-maximising policies.[28] The growing threat to the generation of profits within the corporation will be alleviated, but the old problem of the realisation of profits will return unless profit recipients can be persuaded to spend, rather than hoard, the extra profits they expect to receive.

There still remains the possibility of getting workers to consume more, given that where wage income is relatively high, or has recently been rising fast, workers may choose to save a fraction of their income.[29] If workers can be persuaded to increase their consumption ratio, a realisation crisis could be averted. In a world of underutilised capacity a fall in the saving of workers will imply an increase in profit of precisely the same amount, given the constancy of the other variables in the accounting identity (3.1). The mechanism available to achieve a reduction in saving is via advertising and product innovation. Where wants do not exist, the capitalist system can respond by creating them.[30] Let us therefore examine the ways in which advertising and product innovation may enter the aggregate consumption function.

Duesenberry's problem was 'to find the source of a drive sufficiently strong to account for the amount of work people do, and for the small size of their savings in the face of considerable insecurity' (Duesenberry, 1967, p. 25). In discussing the drive towards higher consumption he cites as an example the average urban family in the USA in 1918 with an income of $1500 (1940 prices) saving 8 per cent of that income, while a 'similarly placed family' in 1941 saved nothing. Duesenberry argues that the desire for saving had not diminished but 'the forces leading to higher consumption increased during that period'. He then relates this to his 'demonstration effect': observing the consumption of others leads to a revised decision about our own level of consumption. However, to explain the drive to higher levels of consumption, the demonstration effect must presuppose its existence and,

rather weakly, Duesenberry asserts that the 'basic source of
the drive toward higher consumption is to be found in the
character of our culture'.[31] Whilst Duesenberry studiously
ignores it, advertising would appear to provide an explanation
for continuing dissatisfaction with our current levels of
consumption, by providing exposure to new goods and creating
new wants and needs. More advertising does not mean more
of the same, but rather information on different and apparently superior goods; that is, advertising cannot be dissociated
from new goods and quality change in established goods. The
demonstration effect can then be seen as *one* mechanism
linking advertising and desired consumption.

Three empirical studies, two for the USA (Yancey, 1958;
Taylor and Weiserbs, 1972) and one for the UK (Peel, 1975)
have demonstrated a significant role for advertising in the
aggregate consumption function. All the other innumerable
empirical studies of the consumption function have not
rejected the hypothesis that advertising matters — they have
simply ignored it. We report below two ordinary least squares
(OLS) regression equations from Peel relating to linear and
linear-in-logarithms specifications, the former implying that
advertising works via autonomous consumption, and the latter
allowing advertising to affect the marginal propensity to
consume. Quarterly data for the period 1956(1) to 1966(4)
for the UK was used in estimation, with advertising (A) being
measured as expenditure on press and television advertising
deflated by a price index for advertising messages (see Cowling
et al., 1975, ch. 3):

$$C_t = -1.1 \times 10^7 + 0.230\ Y_t + 1.644\ A_t - 1.94 \times 10^6 r_t$$
$$\quad (-0.69) \qquad (3.39) \qquad (2.12) \qquad (-2.83)$$
$$\quad + \quad 0.802\ C_{t-1}$$
$$\qquad (11.13)$$

$$R^2 = 0.991$$

$$\ln C_t = 0.700 + 0.393\ \ln Y_t + 0.033\ \ln A_t - 0.021 \ln r$$
$$\quad (2.21) \quad (5.30) \qquad\quad (2.22) \qquad\quad (-2.65)$$
$$\quad + \quad 0.664\ \ln C_{t-1}$$
$$\qquad (9.55)$$
$$R^2 = 0.990$$

C_t and Y_t refer to real consumption and real disposable income, and r_t is the Treasury Bill rate; t-values are in parentheses and the seasonal dummies are not reported. In both formulations the level of real advertising appears to have a significant positive impact on real consumer expenditures, independent of the level of real income. Given that the level of current consumption may have an impact on the level of advertising, a two-equation model in which both advertising and consumption were treated as endogenous variables was also estimated. The results confirmed those of the single-equation model, with all the variables in the consumption function retaining their sign and significance, and suggest an elasticity of consumption w.r.t. advertising of about 0.05 in the short run and 0.07 in the long run. We therefore have some evidence that a doubling of real advertising may raise real consumption by 7 per cent in the long term.[32]

Baran and Sweezy (1966) clearly believe that the impact of selling effort in general is very substantial: 'In its impact on the economy it is outranked only by militarism. In all other aspects of social existence its all pervasive influence is second to none'. But they also regard it as unmeasurable. Whilst not taking that extreme view here, the estimates which have been made have obviously to be taken with a pinch of salt. Looking at the evolution of consumption and advertising over as short a period as ten years is unlikely to reveal 'the basic source of the drive toward higher consumption'. This would require an extended analysis over long periods of capitalist development in a variety of countries. Certainly there has been a secular rise in advertising expenditure which could reconcile the time-series constancy of the consumption ratio with the cross-section observation of its decline as incomes increase. The USA provides the most systematic evidence on the secular tendency (see Table 3.1). It is clear from the evidence that there has been a massive growth in the intensity of advertising over the hundred-year period. Since it is not possible to deflate the series over this extended period, because of the lack of data, it is biased up over time, but this is unlikely to be an important source of error given that the average rate of inflation over the period was probably about one per cent per annum. The second qualification works in the other direction. We have reported the rate of investment in advertising, but the impact of advertising extends over several periods. We should therefore be cumulating advertising expenditures, assuming a rate of depreciation which we expect to be less than 100 per cent p.a. Such a series would obviously show an even stronger tendency to increase over time. The ratio of advertising expenditure to GNP increased through to 1920, fell in the 1930s, and subsequently maintained the same sort of value. The decline since the 1920s disappears if we take the ratio of advertising to personal consumption. What has happened is that state expenditures have grown enormously since then and have taken a much larger share of GNP. The big fall-off of advertising in the Great Depression is real enough, however.

Table 3.1 *Advertising expenditures in the USA 1867—1966*

Year	A ($ millions)	$\dfrac{A}{Y}$
1867	50	0.007
1880	200	0.022
1900	542	0.031
1910	1174	0.032
1920	2935	0.033
1933	1302	0.023
1950	5710	0.020
1960	11932	0.023
1966	16545	0.022

Note: Y is GNP.

Source: Simon (1970, table 7.3, pp. 188—9).

The secular rise in advertising will, following our arguments in Chapter 2, lead to a higher aggregate degree of monopoly, provided its impact on each industry is not washed out by being evenly spread across industries. If it were evenly spread, and its potential impact on consumer behaviour in each industry were similar, then advertising in all markets could increase without having a substantial impact on consumer behaviour in any one.[33] However, if advertising is linked to the other determinants of the degree of monopoly, it would influence the aggregate degree of monopoly in a more substantial way. The theoretical prediction is that advertising will be inversely related to $|\eta|$, the price elasticity of demand, and directly related to α, the degree of collusion over price—output decisions (see Cowling *et al.*, 1975; and J. Cubbin, 1975b),[34] but the relationship with the Herfindahl measure of concentration (H) is expected to have an interior maximum, corresponding to $H \approx 0.4$ in one empirical estimate (see Cable, 1972) and implying that monopolies will tend to pick lower advertising intensities than some oligopolies. However, this implies self-cancelling advertising in the oligopoly case, and therefore the fall-off in total advertising expenditure with monopoly does *not* imply a reduction in the degree of monopoly. The assumption that a monopoly can appropriate all the gains from advertising must mean that efficiency, from the viewpoint of the maximisation of the degree of monopoly, will increase monotonically with H. Thus the general implication is that advertising will vary directly with the degree of monopoly, and therefore there is some presumption that, over time, advertising could accentuate the change in the aggregate degree of monopoly by its correlation with concentration. Oligopolistic sectors of the economy will expand, and also intensify advertising aimed at maximising the profits of the group or industry, whilst competitive sectors will still not advertise.

This basic asymmetry means that higher aggregate levels of advertising will generally imply a higher aggregate degree of monopoly, and in turn a higher degree of monopoly will imply higher levels of advertising. We can therefore conclude that advertising forms part of the mechanism whereby a redistribution from wages to profits is affected. But we have also seen that it appears to provide an antidote to the latent crisis which it has played a part in precipitating. Baran and Sweezy (1966) see advertising as performing a vital role for monopoly capitalism, and to control it would mean that new models, new styles and new ideas would no longer be desired. But these waves of product innovations serve to maintain consumption and expansion. Ironmonger (1970) has sought to document significant innovations in consumer goods since tobacco in the 1630s and has come to the conclusion that the rate of innovation has been increasing over time. His list includes many substantial innovations, e.g. 1840s railways; 1860s sewing machines, dry cleaning; 1870s bicycles, prams, margarine; . . . 1950s television, nylon and terylene fabrics, frozen food, motor scooters, long playing records, colour film, magnetic recording, ballpoint pens, polythene; but it gives no indication of the massive investment in minimal product differentiation of these major innovations. The estimates of Fisher *et al.* (1962) for automobile model change in the USA suggest that the costs involved exceed 25 per cent of the purchase price for this particular consumer good. Some selling costs are indistinguishable from production costs and will therefore be marked up in the usual way, but other product innovation costs and most of the advertising expenditure represent overhead cost and will therefore tend to eat into the share of profits unless the degree of monopoly is, as a consequence, raised by a sufficient degree, or aggregate consumption increases.

The particular problem to be resolved by advertising and product innovation has been the tendency for the propensity to save to increase as real incomes have risen over time. The time-series evidence on the constancy of the consumption ratio would indicate that it has been successful in this regard. Thus it would appear that increased advertising and product innovation could act as an antidote to any underconsumption crisis following a redistribution from wages to profits. However, this would require an increase in selling effort at just such times, whereas advertising may be expected to move procyclically rather than contracyclically: see, for example, Table 3.1, where the 1930s showed a sharp drop in advertising expenditure. Thus although investment in advertising would appear superior to investment in plant and equipment, in that it increases demand without increasing supply and thereby appears to offer a solution to a realisation crisis,[35] the fact that the behaviour of advertising investment follows the behaviour of investment in general quite closely tends to nullify its usefulness.

We conclude at this point that, although there are mechanisms whereby the realisation problems caused by a monopolising economy can be mitigated, by increases in capitalist consumption or investment, increases in managerialism or export surplus, increasing intervention by the state in demand management, or by increased selling effort aimed at reducing the propensity to save, none of these adjustments is automatic, and each of them contains the seeds of possible deeper crisis.[36]

Notes to Chapter 3

1. We are equating gross profits with property income as defined above.
2. We should note here the relationship (previously defined) between Π and Π'. Π' is defined after tax, but includes interest, rent and depreciation payments. Previously $\Pi + F$ was defined as gross capitalist income plus salaries. Thus $\Pi' = (1 - t) (\Pi + F - S - d) - S + d$, where d is depreciation and we assume a constant tax rate on net property income.
3. Some may be surprised by the examples chosen. At least as far as the UK is concerned both the steel industry and the coal industry are largely nationalised and therefore there can be little tendency to further monopolisation. However, it is not entirely far-fetched to lay at least part of the blame for the rapid run-down of the steel industry, and the associated run-down of parts of the coal industry, on the imposition of a profit-maximising (or loss-minimising) pricing policy on the British Steel Corporation. This would appear in our model as an increase in the degree of monopoly.
4. Obviously there will often be substantial uncertainty as to whether the fall in output is temporary or permanent, in which case delaying a decision will tend to be optimal.
5. GEC is a case in point. Following the completion of their monopolisation of significant areas of the electrical engineering industry they failed to invest their profits in the industry and held them in liquid form for some years whilst exploring alternative and mainly foreign outlets (see Dutton, 1980).
6. Clough (1978) provides a useful review of UK studies of the determinants of investment.
7. Oil refining in the USA in the inter-war period was apparently a relatively unconcentrated industry.
8. All sorts of elaborate lag structures could be introduced at this point. It serves our purpose to establish simply that a difference exists between the lag on capacity utilisation and the other two variables.
9. Steindl (1952) and Rowthorn (1979) allow increases in the degree

of monopoly simultaneously to effect profits and capacity utilisation, but the outcome, under plausible assumptions concerning the parameters of the investment function and the savings propensities of capitalists and workers, implies lower levels of profits and capacity utilisation. They are essentially working within a framework defined by $\Pi' = I + C_c$.

10. For a useful review see Lambrinides (1973).

11. Notice that if a redistribution from wages to profits is achieved, and if the increased profits are largely invested in defence of monopoly positions, or indeed in their extension, then, although this may serve to alleviate a short-term crisis, it does not imply a higher rate of equilibrium growth following such a redistribution. Thus in a monopoly or oligopoly world it is no longer the case, even in the long term, that a redistribution favouring profits will allow for a higher growth in wages. Wage increases may bite into capitalist investment, as well as capitalist saving, without necessarily reducing the prospects for the growth of real wages.

12. Such might be said of the UK, where the values and traditions of the landed aristocracy are reflected within the educational institutions and thence in boardrooms and Whitehall. This would appear less true of the US, where a landed aristocracy never secured the same dominance, and of Western Europe, where the bourgeois revolutions were probably more complete.

13. The link between planned investment and retentions policy would seem a more plausible one than the suggested link between the degree of monopoly (price mark-up) and the planned rate of investment (see Eichner, 1976). As argued earlier, it would seem unreasonable to assume that corporations would ever deliberately choose a price—output policy which would restrict the flow of income into the corporation, whatever their plans for the rate of investment. It seems more plausible to assume that they will seek to maximise this flow into the corporation and also minimise the flow out again, subject to the restraints of the capital market.

14. The withholding will be largely from the elements of capital who are external to the corporation. Those elements represented internally will be able to gather the fruits of such policy in other ways. This theme will be taken up later.

15. If the propensity to save out of wages and salaries were greater than zero, this would imply a higher marginal propensity to consume out of gross capitalist income.

16. Marglin (1974) does do some empirical work but it seems better designed to show that transitory income is important in explaining short-run changes in consumption than in demonstrating that the equilibrium ratio of consumption to personal income is one. Certainly he never tries to see whether the consumption ratio is sensitive to the distribution of personal incomes.

17. The basic point, as Lambrinides explains, is that while (external) stockholders have to make some sacrifice in order to secure the

benefits of higher retentions, this is not true of managers if we assume managerial sovereignty. The neoclassical position would be that individual sovereignty prevails and therefore retentions simply reflect the wishes of individuals; stockholders, that is.

18. The significance of the difference, whilst clearly demonstrated in some formulations, was not so clear cut in others. On balance it would seem a reasonable interpretation of Lambrinides's results to say there was evidence of a significant difference.

19. This conclusion would appear plausible, although it requires more rigorous testing. In particular it would be important to estimate a specification of the consumer function which as well as splitting income into personal income and corporate savings, also split personal income into different components.

20. For example, in Chapter 2 we have argued that much of advertising is directed at encouraging brand loyalty and creating dependence, which in turn tends to lead to increasing insensitivity to price changes.

21. This last element is an aspect of internal rather than external control and is closely associated with the struggle between higher- and lower-level management, an aspect of managerialism which we will address in the next chapter.

22. As workers save, so the link between redistribution from wages to profits and a possible realisation crisis is weakened.

23. The marginal propensity to consume of both groups is, however, malleable, and we will turn our attention to this possibility later in the chapter.

24. This theme will be developed in Chapter 5 and 6, which deal with class struggle and international trade.

25. This is not to say that neo-colonial dependency is not still an important attribute of the capitalist system. One only has to recall examples like the dumping on Bangladesh of drugs banned in the West — an interesting example of the response to unplanned excess capacity. The reaction of the tobacco monopolies to falling sales in the West is a further example. Falling sales have undoubtedly been due to publicity about the deadly effects of smoking, and the tobacco monopolies have come to an agreement with the state to restrict advertising and to include health warnings on their promotional materials and the product itself. In contrast, in the Third World they have cynically disregarded the massive evidence on the link between smoking and cancer and promoted their product without restriction or qualification. As a result the Third World is now the big growth area for the consumption of cigarettes and the cancer epidemic has been extended from the West to encompass a growing share of the Third World.

26. If domestic firms were acting as discriminating monopolists with regard to export pricing, then an increased degree of domestic monopoly will leave export prices unchanged so long as marginal cost can be assumed constant within the relevant range of output.

Thus exports would not grow following an increased domestic degree of monopoly.

27. Of course, labour will be required initially to make the new machines, but will not be required (or less will be required) subsequently. It is also possible to envisage a situation where machines become self-reproducing without the intervention of man.

28. This argument will be developed in the context of the rising managerialism associated with the merger boom of the late 1960s and early 1970s discussed in the next chapter.

29. There remains the question of whether the equilibrium propensity to save for most households is significantly less than one. I would agree with Marglin (1974), if we leave aside the very small fraction of households with significant property income, that *equilibrium* consumption ratio is about unity. One of the interesting questions then is, why should this be so? At this point we are merely saying that workers will not immediately consume everything they earn, especially in circumstances where their earnings have been increasing quite rapidly, and perhaps erratically.

30. This, of course, applies to all households and not just to worker households.

31. He tries to pin this down by (a) associating status and income (and relates these to consumption — the *non-sequitur*), and (b) by recognising the general goal of higher living standards; but neither implies higher levels of consumption of consumption goods (as opposed to leisure and power).

32. Whether we can say much about what would happen if advertising were doubled is debatable, but the specification (linear-in-logarithms) does imply diminishing returns to advertising.

33. The impact on *aggregate* consumption would remain, however, and this could be consistent with some increase in the aggregate degree of monopoly in such cases.

34. These predictions follow from an extended version of the Dorfman-Steiner condition for profit-maximising advertising and price policies, where the advertising intensity is set equal to the ratio of advertising to price elasticity of demand.

35. See the interesting article on this by Rothschild (1942).

36. This also applies to advertising and the creation of wants. Should the system ever fail to satisfy such enhanced wants then the consequences in terms of social disruption and breakdown will be that much more severe.

4

Mergers and Managerialism

Having examined the link between monopolisation and the share of profits in the economy, we now turn to examine the process of monopolisation itself and its apparent impact within a managerial world. It is clear that the post-war period, and especially the late 1960s and early 1970s, have been characterised by a dramatic change in the structure of the capitalist sector of the economy. This has come about via large-scale merger activity, which in Europe at least has been principally horizontal in character — that is, it involved the joining together of corporations to form new giants which dominated specific industries or sectors of the economy (see Aaronovitch and Sawyer, 1975; Hannah and Kay, 1977; Prais, 1976). The situation in the USA was somewhat different since the anti-trust laws largely prohibited horizontal mergers. Merger activity was still commonplace, however, and new giant corporations were formed; these were generally conglomerate in character, although the dominance of these giants in any one market is partly determined by their very size — whether in that specific market or beyond.

To get an idea of the magnitude of merger activity we report some aggregate estimates for the UK for the period 1954—75 in Table 4.1. The data are not comparable over the full period because prior to 1966 they relate only to mergers between quoted companies in manufacturing, whereas post 1966 they essentially cover all consummated mergers involving assets acquired in excess of £5 million. Thus the series covers only the larger acquisitions, the total number of mergers being very much larger; for example, press reports indicated a total of 884 mergers in 1971 in contrast to the 110 reported

in Table 4.1. The series therefore is likely to understate substantially the true level of merger activity, but
may nevertheless provide a fairly accurate indication of trends
in the two periods.[1] This is confirmed by estimates reported
by Meeks (1977) for the 893 companies which continued in
independent existence within the Department of Industry
quoted company population, 1949—69.

Table 4.1   *Merger activity, UK (1954—75)*

	Net assets acquired (£ million)	Number of acquisitions
1954	77	35
1955	62	37
1956	61	33
1957	103	58
1958	114	52
1959	148	72
1960	257	77
1961	323	67
1962	183	53
1963	152	59
1964	180	52
1965	257	48
1966	998	63
1967	2273	96
1968	8499	133
1969	3714	126
1970	2598	80
1971	1687	110
1972	3588	114
1973	4870	134
1974	7621	141
1975	5786	160

Sources: 1954—65 Utton (1969); 1966—75 Office of Fair Trading.

Despite being an understatement of the true position the
data still reveal the massive proportions of the merger wave
of the late 1960s. Taking 1968, a year of peak merger activity,
which is confirmed by Meeks, we see that expenditure on
acquisitions (£8,499 million) exceeded gross domestic fixed
capital formation (£8,097 million) and was almost double the
net figure (£4,444 million). Perhaps more significantly,

expenditure on acquisitions in that year implied the takeover of 27 per cent of the capital stock of the companies sector of the total economy (companies sector fixed assets were valued at £31,500 million in 1968)! This was of course a peak year, but we should also remember that our estimate understates the magnitude of merger activity, and the other years of the late 1960s and early 1970s imply an annual rate of takeover of very significant fractions of the total private capital stock of the economy. Of course, there may be an element of double counting if big fish eat little fish and in their turn they are themselves eaten up by bigger fish, but such double counting *within a year* is likely to be slight, since an acquirer (being a pretty big fish) would not be immediately acquired. However, we would expect this to go on over a period, and to illustrate this, and to give a feel for the impact of all this merger activity on particular sectors of the economy, we detail the history of two giants created in 1968, British Leyland Motor Corporation and the General Electric Company (GEC): see Figures 4.1 and 4.2 (overleaf), which are the work of John Cubbin and Pat Dutton respectively. In each case the 1968 merger represented the culmination of a series of mergers extending back through the 1960s, and in some cases much earlier, in which most of the major British capital interests in the motor car and electrical engineering industries respectively were brought together into one giant firm.[2]

Clearly British Leyland and GEC were examples of horizontal merger, with firms operating in the same markets joining together, but this was the general case in the late 1960s. Office of Fair Trading statistics reveal that in 1968, 82 per cent of mergers were horizontal, and these represented 91 per cent by value.[3] 1968 was typical of the whole period 1965–70, but less so for the period 1971–5, when the proportion of diversified mergers appeared to increase. In this later period the proportion of horizontal mergers had fallen to around 70 per cent by number and rather less by value. Whilst we can accept this as a tendency, and indeed beyond a point opportunities for horizontal merger must begin to dry up, there remains the question as to whether or not the statistics accurately classify mergers to one category or another. An examination of individual cases suggests that Merger Panel

Figure 4.1 *The history of the British Leyland Motor Corporation (BLMC)*

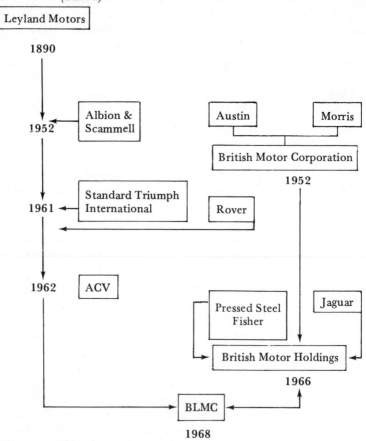

Source: Cowling *et al.* (1980, ch. 6).

statistics are based on rather narrow industry definitions and thus it is quite possible for a merger to be classified as diversified when in fact the firms involved are operating in fairly closely related markets, e.g. 'traditional' versus 'newer' domestic appliances; diamond abrasive wheels versus cutting tools; different types of goods supplied to builders' merchants; and subsectors of the ethical pharmaceutical industry. It is therefore at least arguable that the proportion of merger classified as horizontal understates the true position. This is of some importance because changes in the degree of monopoly will be more directly related to horizontal mergers than to diversified mergers. It would seem reasonable to conclude, on the basis of the evidence presented, that the vast majority of acquisitions during the merger boom in the late 1960s were of the horizontal variety, and therefore contributed to the monopolisation of markets, and that this was still true in the 1970s, despite the evidence of some trend toward diversified merger. This would therefore seem an appropriate point at

Figure 4.2 *The history of the General Electric Company (GEC)*

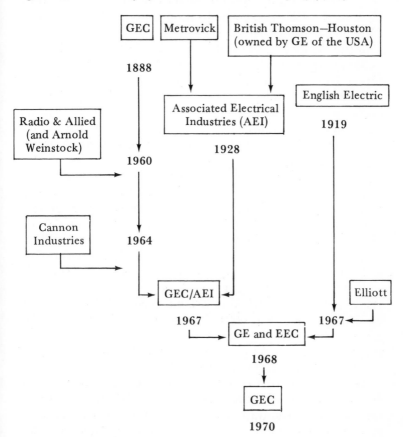

Source: Cowling *et al.* (1980, ch. 6).

which to consider the growth in aggregate and market concentration and the contribution of the merger wave to that growth.

Aggregate concentration, as measured by the share of the hundred largest enterprises in manufacturing net output, has risen very rapidly over the post-war period after remaining fairly stable over the interwar period and falling somewhat during the Second World War. Prais (1976) estimated that in 1949 the top hundred firms had a 20 per cent share which rose to 40 per cent by 1970, an increase which was not paralleled in the USA. It is also clear that the current level of concentration cannot be explained by plant size, either in the USA or the UK. The concentration ratio of the largest hundred plants has remained stable at 9 or 10 per cent in both countries over an extended period, implying the widespread existence of multiplant operation. The 200 largest manufacturing enterprises in the USA had an average of 45 plants each in 1963, whilst the 100 largest enterprises in the UK averaged 27 plants in 1958, rising to 72 plants in 1972. At the same time employment per plant for these giant enterprises fell from 750 employees in 1958 to 430 employees in 1972.

Using data on quoted companies, Prais also estimated the relative importance of merger and internal growth to changes in aggregate concentration. His results suggest that mergers were of supreme importance for the periods 1919–30 and 1957–69, but probably unimportant in between. About three-quarters of the increase in concentration between 1919 and 1930 was probably due to merger, and between 1957 and 1969 more than 100 per cent of the increase can be attributed to merger.[4] This is confirmed in estimates made by Hannah and Kay (1977), but for a slightly different period, 1958–67, whereas Aaronovitch and Sawyer (1975) conclude that only 54 per cent of the growth in concentration for the top 100 was due to merger.[5]

Turning to market concentration, a central problem is the definition of a market: the narrower the definition, the higher the level of concentration will generally be. The other major problem is that market share data are not generally accessible, the Census of Production limiting the available information to a specific concentration ratio, usually the five-firm ratio (i.e. the ratio of the output, or sales or employment, of the biggest five enterprises to that of the industry in question).[6] There are also problems with comparisons over time using census data because of changes in industry definitions and in the level at which the concentration ratio is defined, usually either minimum list heading (three digit) or product group (four digit). We will provide some estimates from Hannah and Kay (1977) of the level and growth in concentration for very broad categories within manufacturing, together with estimates of the proportion of the observed growth which was due to merger, and some estimates of concentration in a range of specific product markets. We will then give two examples of the evolution of concentration within specific product markets.

Table 4.2 details 10-firm concentration ratios (CR_{10}) for 1957 and 1969 and an estimate of the proportion of the change in CR_{10} due to merger for broad industry groups in manufacturing. Eleven industry groups revealed an increased level of concentration over the period, two showed a decline and one showed no change.[7] Because the industries refer to very broad categories, like food or metal manufacture, it would be possible to have every reasonably defined market within each group completely monopolised and still get a quite low value for CR_{10}. It is also true that significant mergers between major firms within a specific industry will have little impact on CR_{10} if the marginal firm drawn into the top 10 net is relatively small. Thus the table gives only a limited guide to what is going on within a particular industry, but, subject to these major qualifications, a picture is presented of widespread and substantial increases in concentration over the period in question, with merger accounting for most of the increase in all cases except one. In fact for five of the industry groups merger accounts for more than 100 per cent of the change, implying that internal growth was a deconcentrating force in these cases.

As we have already noted, except in the case of tobacco (where the CR_{10} is 100 per cent in both 1957 and 1969), the industries identified in Table 4.2 are far too broad to indicate the degree of concentration in any specific product market. From Chapter 2 we can also recall that the measure of

Table 4.2 *Merger and market concentration: UK manufacturing 1957–69*

Industry	CR_{10} 1957	CR_{10} 1969	% change due to merger
Food	62.1	80.5	70.1
Drink	40.8	87.2	76.3
Tobacco	100.0	100.0	–
Chemicals	80.6	86.4	31.2
Metal manufacture	58.7	74.3	107.01
Non-electrical engineering	39.0	32.1	–
Electrical engineering	60.4	81.2	105.8
Shipbuilding	80.3	93.3	80.8
Vehicles and aircraft	57.2	85.8	70.6
Metal goods n.e.s.	67.2	77.1	129.2
Textiles	55.9	74.2	127.8
Building materials	71.2	65.0	–
Paper and publishing	63.6	78.1	111.1
Miscellaneous	58.3	65.6	95.9

n.e.s. = not elsewhere specified.
Source: Hannah and Kay (1977).

concentration entering the determination of the degree of monopoly $[(p - mc)/p]$ in our formulation is the Herfindahl measure (H), which is the sum of squared market shares of all the firms comprising the industry, $\sum_i (X_i/X)^2$. Despite much prompting from academic industrial economists, the Office of Business Statistics has refused to provide estimates of H derived from the Census of Production returns, so that researchers have had to try and estimate them on the basis of only limited information on market shares. To give some idea of the size of H in an array of fairly well defined markets for household products, we detail estimates made by John Cable from brand market-share data in Table 4.3. We also provide estimates of the four-firm concentration ratio (CR_4) and the intensity of advertising (A/R). It is clear that most of these markets were already highly concentrated by 1963, the year to which the market share information relates. Taking the first product, margarine, as an example, we can see that the Herfindahl index is greater than for a symmetric duopoly,[8] and the top four firms account for 97 per cent of the market.

This is an extreme example, but for 24 products out of the 27 listed the top four firms accounted for a majority of sales, and for 17 out of the 27 they accounted for more than three-quarters. This is all prior to the significant merger activity of the late 1960s and early 1970s. We can also see that advertising, and the data relate only to press and television advertising, also absorbs a significant fraction of sales revenue — in the case of toilet soap almost a quarter!

Table 4.3 *Concentration and advertising in an array of UK markets for household products*

Product	H	CR_4	A/R (%)
Margarine	0.59	97	7.6
Instant coffe	0.39	82	9.4
Salt	0.44	82	0.7
Baked beans	0.51	89	2.5
Biscuits	0.07	39	2.3
Canned soups	0.48	91	3.2
Evaporated and condensed milk	0.27	79	3.5
Flour	0.30	78	2.4
Jam	0.17	64	1.9
Table jelly	0.25	76	1.4
Packeted cheese	0.54	84	4.7
Breakfast cereals	0.40	89	11.0
Sausages	0.07	33	1.3
Canned fish	0.08	39	1.0
Cake mix	0.38	92	10.3
Meat extract	0.50	95	14.1
Sugar	0.40	82	0
Cigarettes	0.43	94	1.0*
Toothpaste	0.14	63	12.0
Lipstick	0.10	45	9.5
Face powder	0.18	64	11.2
Soap and detergents	0.41	90	13.7
Shoe polish	0.41	89	14.3
Toilet soap	0.14	57	24.0
Disinfectants	0.13	56	6.1
Household bleach	0.36	81	5.5
Household polish	0.24	73	13.8

* This ratio is misleadingly small because R includes tobacco duty.
Source: John Cable, upublished estimates.

Whilst Table 4.3 provides an interesting snapshot at a point in time in the evolution of concentration (and advertising) as it relates to the market for specific household products, it gives no indication of how such markets are being restructured, whereas Table 4.2 outlined the trend towards concentration but for broad definitions of industry and concentration — the ten-firm concentration ratio. To get more of a feel for what was going on in specific industries we cite the cases of brewing and textiles.[9]

Table 4.4   *Market shares in the brewing industry (1974)*

	Market share (%)	Number of outlets
Bass Charrington	20	10946
Allied	16	9750
Whitbread	12	8964
Watneys	14	8100
Scottish & Newcastle	9	1770
Courage	9	6900

Source: Cowling *et al.* (1980).

The recent history of the brewing industry reveals a dramatic fall in both breweries and brewing companies. In 1939 there were 1418 breweries owned by 559 brewing companies, but by 1960 the number of breweries had fallen to 358 and companies to 247. Between 1960 and 1973 the number of companies was cut by two-thirds to 88, and the number of breweries by more than half to 162, with the decline being almost entirely due to merger. However, this still gives a false impression of structural change in the industry, where six giants have been created which dominate the industry (see Table 4.4). These six firms control about 80 per cent of the market, in terms of both production and distribution via the tied-house system, whilst the other 82 small regional brewers collectively provide the other 20 per cent. But in terms of the monopolisation of markets which are meaningful as far as the consumer is concerned, this still gives a false impression of the evolution and present structure of the industry. All market shares given are national, but for the individual beer drinker it is little comfort to know that there are still **88** brewers, or even six majors, when all the pubs in the immediate vicinity are controlled by one or two of them.

Another example of the restructuring of an industry over recent history is the case of textiles, which was transformed mainly by the activities of one company, Courtaulds. Before the 1960s Courtaulds' predominant interest was in man-made fibres, particularly rayon, but in the course of the 1960s and 1970s the company initiated a continuous stream of mergers with firms operating in various segments of the textile industry and emerged in a position of dominance in most sectors. According to Knight (1974), over the period 1962–9, £175 million was spent on acquisitions, of which £146 million was spent on acquisitions in the textile industry. These included at least forty-seven separate major acquisitions (see Cowling *et al.*, 1980). As an example of a fairly hectic year, in 1964 Courtaulds acquired two very large spinning companies, Fine Spinners and Doublers for about £12 million and the Lancashire Cotton Corporation for more than £16 million, together with six other major firms. By mid-1968 Courtaulds' market share of the spinning industry had reached 30 per cent; of filament weaving, 22 per cent; and of warp knitting, 35 per cent; all from nothing in 1962.

These two examples of dramatic structural transformation of industries in recent history, by the creation of giant firms via a process of intensive merger activity over an extended period, is typical of the industrial scene in general, as we have seen earlier. Thus the evidence points to merger as promoting market concentration, but was this in fact the motivation for merger, or simply an inevitable consequence of amalgamation for reasons of efficiency? *A priori* it would seem that both objectives would be potentially relevent to any profit-seeking capitalist enterprise, but Newbould (1970) went and asked the managers involved — with some rather surprising results. The results of his interviews give striking confirmation of the view that the elimination of competition (market dominance) was the most important single motive for merger. In contrast, technological reasons (e.g. scale economies) appeared to be a minor motive. The results are perhaps surprising given that merging in order to secure scale economies is likely to be deemed more socially acceptable than merging in order to reduce competition. If anything therefore Newbould's results are likely to understate the true position regarding merger to secure dominance, and overstate the technological reasons.

Given the historical record it is evident that the merger movement has been the main vehicle for the monopolisation of markets in the post-war period,[10] and it is also reasonable to conclude, not least because of the declared motivation of those involved, that it has also been the prime force leading to an increase in the degree of monopoly within these economies.[11] However, despite this, studies of the impact of merger have been fairly unambiguous in reporting a reduction in the rate of profit as a consequence of merger. Singh (1971), examining the experience of the 1950s, reported a decline in relative profitability following merger and that the decline was not reversed in the longer term. Utton (1974) made a comparison of merger-intensive firms with their industry average and found the profit rate for more than half to be below the industry median. He also found that merger-intensive firms were less profitable than non-merger-intensive firms. Meeks's (1977) large-scale statistical study revealed a significant decline in profit rate in the first five years post-merger, but this decline was not significant in the sixth and seventh years. His results are after allowing for accounting bias due to the revaluation of the merged firm, and after making comparisons with the industry average, although the industries were, of necessity, broadly based.[12] The various UK investigations of the relationship between the rate of profit and the size of firm, culminating with the article by Whittington (1980), all point in the same direction: if there is any relationship between profit rate and size, and the relationship generally is quite weak, then it is negative.

The evidence therefore strongly suggests that, despite the fact that we may expect an increase in the degree of market control following merger, and, by such means, an increase in the degree of monopoly, we are nevertheless observing a relative decline in the rate of profit for those firms which are growing rapidly via merger. Similarly those firms which are relatively large, and may therefore be expected to possess a greater degree of market control, do not appear to have generated higher rates of return on capital. Reconciliation of expectation and observation must come from a recognition that costs, particularly overhead costs, as well as the degree of monopoly, will be affected by both the process and outcome of merger activity. In the short term transition costs incident to the integration of two or more corporations into one centrally controlled unit can be expected. In the longer term we may expect that the dramatic change in both the size and complexity of the giant corporation will pose problems of efficiency and control, particularly where this change is imposed on an organisational base which was quite inappropriate.

The dominant organisational form in Britain in the 1950s and early 1960s, prior to the major merger wave, was either the functionally organised, unitary form structure (U-form) or the holding company (H-form) (see Channon, 1973; Steer, 1979). The U-form firm consisted of a single, hierarchical structure organised on a functional basis (eg. manufacturing, finance, marketing), with each function being represented in capital allocation decisions, whereas the H-form comprised an unco-ordinated group of companies falling under a single financial entity. As U-form companies grew through merger, so they developed larger and more cumbersome hierarchies with increasing problems of communication and control. This can be expected to lead to increasingly dysfunctional behaviour at various levels of the managerial hierarchy, coupled with inefficient strategic decision-making (see, for example, Williamson, 1970). Excessive staff and managerial slack at each level of the hierarchy will induce imitative consequences among lower-level staff, and the presence of functional heads in strategic decision-making will introduce biases and inefficiency given that their position will be at least partly dictated by their own empire-building objectives. In the case of H-form organisations, growth through merger implied they simply became larger, more sprawling and more ill-coordinated empires.

The answer to the problems of internal control posed by these giant organisations, which were spawned as an answer to problems of market control, was seen to lie in the decentralisation of responsibility for production, coupled with the centralisation of capital allocation decisions. These properties were captured in the multi-divisional structure (M-form), which had been innovated by Dupont and General Motors in the USA as far back as the 1920s, and it was this organisational form which was increasingly adopted by the giant British corporations in the late 1960s and 1970s. The M-form structure achieved the separation of short-run operational decision-making from long-term strategic decision-making by the creation of a general office, quite independent of production divisions, with the objective of establishing an efficient internal capital market based on the reported profitability of operating divisions. Thus the board, operating via the general office, would be able to re-establish some degree of control over the flow of profits within the corporation. The efficiency of such a system would itself reflect the power of the board and its associated higher-level executives, who themselves will often have a considerable stake in the equity, relative to the power of lower-level divisional management. The introduction of the M-form structure represents a process whereby higher level management removes itself from direct supervision of the generation of profits, but uses as a sanction its control over capital flows. Divisional managers are controlled by a competitive and relatively well-informed capital market and thus the propensity of such managers to absorb profits rather than report them is severely curtailed. The M-form organisation should be seen therefore as a relatively efficient mechanism for extracting profit from operating divisions, and thereby minimising managerial discretion at that level. It should also be seen as an efficient structure for making long-term strategic decisions because it does not suffer from the biases introduced by the presence of functional divisions and because of the qualitative (and quantitative) change in the information going through to the peak co-ordinator's office, which is no longer crowded out with input related to day-to-day decision-making and can therefore focus more sharply on strategic issues. Thus we could expect profitability to rise for these two main reasons, and to this extent the M-form structure would allow the re-emergence of cost-minimising behaviour. The importance of the innovation would then be conditional on the extent of the departure from cost-minimising behaviour in the existing managerial world with its U-form or H-form structures.

Williamson (1964) provides two types of empirical evidence on the extent of managerial discretion. First he reports case-study responses by individual firms to situations of adversity. To take a hypothetical case in point, 'Chemical Products', he assesses the impact of a two-year programme of cost reduction. He found that, *with no change in the rate of output*, the rate of return on capital went up 125 per cent, salaried employees went down 32 per cent and headquarters employment went down by 40 per cent. He also details the rather dramatic reductions in associated staff expenses. Thus the advent of peculiar and serious conditions of adversity surrounding this particular firm revealed the existence of massive overstaffing within the managerial hierarchy, which contributed to a very significant reduction in the rate of profit. This picture is repeated in the various cases investigated by Williamson, and provides a glimpse of the exent of unreported profits which are normally hidden from view. This does not mean of course that management in these organisations is not interested in cost control. Ignoring the struggle within the managerial hierarchy, it is clear that management has a different attitude towards some costs than towards others. Williamson has characterised this as expense preference, and identifies staff and associated expenses as contributing directly to managerial utility. This still leaves the minimisation of the direct costs of production as an objective of management, since profits are still desirable for their own sake and as a source of those elements of (overhead) costs for which management has an expense preference. Managerialism should therefore be identified with the adoption of profit-maximising rules with regard to short-run output–price determination, but also with the absorption of profits within various categories of overhead costs. Williamson investigates a specific element of overhead costs, the salary of the chief executive, and finds that doubling the concentration ratio is associated with a 50 per cent increase in the salary of the chief executive, after controlling for the size of the firm and the degree of managerial control. He argues, based on earlier work by Simon (1957), that the salary of the chief executive will accurately reflect the general level of salaries and expects the same sort of relationship to hold for non-pecuniary managerial income. This finding strongly suggests that management is able to siphon off a considerable proportion of the extra profits implicit in a higher degree of market control, so that at the limit we might observe firms in monopoly positions apparently being no more profitable than firms in more competitive markets. This sort of finding receives support from a study of airline efficiency (Gordon, 1965). Efficiency was found to be inversely related to the degree of monopoly (i.e. favourable route advantage) and difference in efficiency were primarily due to excess overhead personnel. These differences were non-trivial — if only one-third of potential cost savings were achieved the rate of return on capital would be doubled.

An alternative source of evidence on the importance of managerial discretion is provided by those studies which have investigated the inter-firm relationship between profitability and control type, typically owner or managerial control, defined in some rather arbitrary fashion but based on a measure of the diffusion of share ownership and/or the representation of management on the board. The earlier studies of Kamerschen (1968), Monsen, Chiu and Cooley (1958) and Larner (1970) involved specification errors arising from their failure to recognise that managerial control is not sufficient for the existence of a significant degree of discretionary activity. The effect of control type — managerial or owner control — will be conditional on the degree of monopoly power, as our earlier analysis suggested. This probably explains the mixed results obtained. Monsen, Chiu and Cooley show a significant and substantial difference in the rate of return on capital between owner-controlled firms and others, Larner found a slight difference, while Kamerschen found no significant difference.[13] However, a more recent study by Palmer (1973) allows for the interaction between the degree of monopoly and control type and finds that only with a high degree of monopoly power does management control result in a significantly lower average profit rate.[14] With strong owner-control and a high degree of monopoly power, he finds an average reported profit rate of 14.8 per cent, whereas with the same degree of monopoly power the management-controlled group revealed an average reported rate of profit of 11.4 per cent, a difference which appeared highly significant. He also checked for reasons for low profit rates in the managerially controlled group and came to the conclusion that in most cases the firms in question were similar in all respects, except for control type, to other firms with high profits in the same industry.

It would therefore appear that the absorption of profits in a managerial world can be a very significant phenomenon, so that the innovation of an efficient internal control structure would seem a potentially significant innovation, and indeed the impact of control type, reviewed above, is likely to include the impact of the M-form innovation. However, whilst the M-form organisation may be an efficient mechanism for the extraction of profits from operating divisions, and thereby minimising managerial discretion at that level, there remains the question of the absorption of profits by the general office. Managerialism as a problem for external capital remains in so far as the propensity of the general office to absorb profits remains, even though they may be substantial equity holders, given that an extra million pounds diverted to salaries or internal consumption (i.e. various non-pecuniary benefits) will be generally more beneficial to those comprising the general office than would an extra million reported as profits, which would be divided many ways, among stockholders completely outside the corporation as well as to those who are its internal controllers.[15] However, absorption of profits at the level of the general office is going to be limited by the very transparency of the process — the general office is basically distinct and identifiable from the rest of the organisation and its expenditure can be perhaps readily observed. This is not to say that such absorption cannot be considerable. It seems that Henry Ford II may have recently overstepped the bounds of what was considered reasonable and inspired a stockholders' revolt. Their action cites the equipping of his office with a $250,000 sauna, private gym and full-time masseur, and a private dining-room for him and his guests, staffed with six full-time employees including a Swiss chef. Each lunch that Ford eats was alleged to cost approximately

$200 per person. Ford was also accused of having five to six company employees tend his girlfriend's lawn, along with various other indiscretions and misuses of funds (*Morning Star*, 3 March 1979). Similar sorts of gastronomical indulgences were revealed in UK firms by Polly Toynbee (*Guardian*, 11 February 1980). Her investigations revealed that 'In the City and big companies all over the country good eating is part of the rich fabric of everyday top management life.' She quotes the person in charge of one boardroom dining-room as saying she has an unlimited budget for food, she can have whatever kitchen equipment she desires, and that service is from 'silver salvers, beautiful silver coffee pots, silver cigar and cigarette boxes and lovely cut glasses'. But she says also that hers is not the grandest dining-room in the building: 'the chairman has an even grander one, with grander food, a butler and Georgian furniture'. Another person involved in these activities sent 'girls with hampers to Ascot, Wimbledon, Glyndebourne and Twickenham' and 'cooks to company holidays — chalets in Switzerland, shooting parties in the Highlands, trips to villas in the Bahamas'. There are obviously lots of ways in which profits can be absorbed within the upper reaches of the managerial hierarchy, but in addition we can also expect the controlling internal group to set the retention ratio above a level which external capital would wish to see, and this can be managed with a quite small minority shareholding.[16]

In terms of our model, then, $(\pi^* + F)/Y$ will tend to rise as merger contributes to an increase in the degree of monopoly, but π/Y (the share of reported profits) will tend to fall if overhead costs rise sufficiently. Managerialism, plus the purely technical transition costs, will tend to lead to higher overhead costs in these giant organisations, at least until some more appropriate form of internal organisation is introduced. In the USA the multi-divisional firm, although inaugurated in the 1920s, first became of quantitative importance in the early post-war period, diffusing rapidly across large industrial corporations in the 1950s and forming the basis of the conglomerate organisations of the 1960s, so that by 1969 the multi-divisional structure had been adopted by about 80 per cent of the 500 major corporations (Rumelt, 1974). In contrast with the US experience the innovation has been very much delayed within Europe. Of the top 100 firms in the UK only 2½ per cent had adopted the multi-divisional structure by 1950 (and most of these were subsidiaries of US companies), in contrast to about 25 per cent of the top 500 firms in the USA. It was not until the late 1960s that things really began to change quite fast, so that by 1970 about 57.5 per cent had adopted (Chandler and Daems, 1974). The pattern of change was similar in France and Germany (Chandler and Daems, 1974).

As far as the UK was concerned, most of the big companies called in outside management consultants to advise on restructuring, and in most of these cases the consultant firm was McKinsey and Company, an American company which nearly always recommended a form of multi-divisional organisation that had proved successful in the USA (Channon, 1973). However, some of the UK organisational structures so created proved to be very pale imitations of the American model, with divisional managers still participating in strategic decision-making and general officers still involved in operational decisions (Channon, 1973). This is likely to reflect the lag in adoption of the new structure and we may expect a move of the UK towards the US version as time passes.

The significance of the multi-divisional innovation is emphasised in some recent work by Steer and Cable (1978). Using UK firm data for the period 1967—71, regressions of the rate of return on capital on firm characteristics and dummy variables representing organisational form and organisational change were estimated. Their equations reveal a difference in the rate of profit of six to nine percentage points for the optimal form of internal organisation (normally the M-form) compared with alternative forms (normally either H-form or U-form), after controlling for a variety of other determinants of the rate of profit. This result is, of course, quantitatively very important, revealing an increase in profit rate of up to almost 100 per cent in response to internal reorganisation aimed at establishing control over costs.[17] The only other comprehensive published study, by Armour and Teece (1978) for the US oil industry, confirms these results. They found that over the 1955—68 period the multi-divisional organisational structure raised the rate of return on stockholders' equity by about two percentage points above the 7½ per cent level realised by the functionally organised firm. This is less than the difference between optimally and sub-optimally organised firms recorded by Steer and Cable for the UK, but this is consistent with the longer history of the M-form in the USA which has allowed more firms to pick the optimal form of organisation and therefore narrow the observed differences in profitability between observed organisational forms. Thus we can expect to see the big differences in the period of early diffusion of organisational innovations and these differences can be expected to taper off as the diffusion curve reaches its asymptote. This view receives support from the results reported by Armour and Teece for the later period they examine, 1969—73, when they are unable to detect any difference between rates of return for different organisational forms. Apparently the diffusion process was complete and all firms had adopted the organisational form appropriate to their circumstances — essentially the smaller oil corporations had retained a functional organisation whilst the giants had adopted the multi-divisional structure. Unfortunately Armour and Teece argue that differential performance would not be observable in this later period 'since the efficiency gains would have been passed on to consumers rather than having been impounded as profits' (p. 119). This is simply not the case, since the average rate of return for the M-form firms in their sample had risen from about 9½ per cent in the period 1956—68 to 14 per cent in 1969—73. What the innovation had done was to raise the level of efficiency in the giant functionally organised firms to that achieved by their smaller rivals, thus raising the average rate of profit for the industry as a whole.[18]

We can therefore see the multi-divisional organisational form as an adaptive response by top-level, equity-holding management to the growing encroachment on profits of discretionary behaviour by lower-level management, given the opportunities offered by the emergence of the giant, complex, ill-co-ordinated empires thrown up by the merger wave of the late 1960s and 1970s. The magnitude of the response over this period is indicated in Steer and Cable (1978). In their sample of 120 of the largest companies in the UK, the number having a holding-company structure went down from about 37 to 14 between the periods 1964—6 and 1970—2, that is between the period immediately prior to the big merger wave and a period in the middle of that wave. At the same time there was a reduction in U-form enterprises from 14 to 9. The H-form and U-form structures were replaced by a variety of M-form structures. The pure M-form went up from 21 to 35, but, most dramatically, the number of firms with transitional M-form structures went up from 12 to 40. At the same time the corrupted M-form (M-form control apparatus but central management overinvolved in operating affairs) declined substantially from 17 to 7.

Thus the period was one of widescale and comprehensive reorganisation within the corporate structures of the UK economy. The empirical evidence suggests that the M-form organisation represented a very significant innovation and gives considerable support to Williamson's view that it was 'American capitalism's most important single innovation of the 20th century', and he therefore infers that 'experience does not seem to spell capitalism's early bureaucratic demise'. However, although he poses the problem in efficiency terms, the essence of the problem is clearly distributional — a struggle between a controlling group of owner-managers and the rest of the managerial hierarchy over the flow of profits generated within the corporation. The innovation is therefore analogous to that of the factory system in the eighteenth and nineteenth centuries. As Marglin (1974) argues, the initial impetus for the innovation of the factory was distributional rather than technological. It was seen as an appropriate response to the lack of effort and embezzlement by the independent spinners and weavers of the putting-out system. What was wanted was an organisational system which would secure a higher level of effort and provide control over embezzlement. The factory was the answer then; the M-form structure of the modern corporation is seen as an answer now to the analogous problem of discretionary behaviour within the managerial hierarchy. It is clear, as Marglin pointed out in reference to feudal society and collectivisation in the Soviet Union, that 'the resort of economically and politically powerful classes to innovation in order to change the distribution of income in their favour (rather than to increase its size) was not unique to the industrial revolution'.

We conclude that managerialism, and the capitalist response to it, have to be recognised as important phenomena in any attempt to explain changes in the revealed profit rate in economies which are being structurally transformed. During the early years of the merger wave overhead costs, due to the discretionary activity of management, were getting out of hand. The capitalist response was the innovation of the M-form structure which re-established control of over-head costs *within* the managerial hierarchy, but not at its apex. Nevertheless profitability was raised, the remaining major problem for external capital being its inability to get hold of the increased profit flow generated by such internal control policies, given that retentions policy will remain in the hands of a controlling group, which can exist with a quite small fraction of the total stock, and which is itself within the corporation and therefore a recipient of the benefits to be had from profits absorbed or retained within the corporate structure.

It is necessary to emphasise that there is nothing in our argument that would lead to the conclusion that the advent of managerial capitalism implies the end of class struggle. Nothing could be further from the truth. Most managerialists have emphasised the growing divorcement of ownership from control as the increasing diffusion of share-ownership has left management in control, and this has in turn radically changed the working of the capitalist system. Some have proclaimed the advent of the 'soulful corporation', and more generally there has been a fairly widespread assumption that the interests of management are not in conflict with those of workers (see, for example, Kaysen, 1957, and Crosland, 1962). But neither basic assumption has much to commend it. Although legal ownership has become increasingly separated from control, the dominant group of big capitalists has retained control from within the corporations. They are also managers, but they have the same interests as capitalists always had — the extraction of as large a volume of profits as possible from the resources they control. This does not mean that all profits will be reported as such, since some will be siphoned off by top management in the pursuit of its own objectives. And neither does it mean that the corporations will be run with the welfare of external holders of stock in mind, since retentions will usually be beyond the levels consistent with external stockholder welfare. What it does mean is that such managerial corporations will seek to minimise the direct costs of production, and therefore wage costs, and will choose price—output levels which maximise profits. Thus by way of wages, productivity and prices the managerial capitalist system will act to exploit labour within the sphere of distribution, production, and through the markets. The fruits of such exploitation will appear in the profits produced but also in various elements of overhead costs. Thus managerialism will not act to moderate the impact of a rising degree of monopoly by picking output rates beyond the profit-maximising level. It will have more of a distributional effect than an allocative effect, having less to do with what is produced and how much is produced, and more to do with who receives the profits from such production.

There remains the question of the link between managerialism and the realisation of profits. Managerialism reduces the reported profit rate by raising overheads, but may act as an antidote to crisis by raising 'capitalist' consumption. In this sense the M-form innovation has ambiguous effects in aggregate. A differential can exist between the profit rate for those corporations which have innovated and those which have not, and yet the profit rate on average could fall if, as a result, the level of capacity utilisation were to fall. The capitalist response to managerialism may re-pose the question of the realisation of profits. Thus, whilst for a given output every increase in discretionary expenditure must reduce profits by an equal amount, under conditions of excess capacity managers can *in aggregate* earn what they spend — managerialism can be self-financing. However, within the context of the recent history of the UK it appears that managerialism posed a problem for capital before the question of realisation did. Merger was leading to lower profit rates, despite the expected increased degree of monopoly. It appears that increased managerial discretion actually exceeded the monopoly profits implicit in the typical merger so that profits would have fallen even though a realisation crisis might have been avoided. It follows that innovations to contain and reduce managerialism would, under such conditions, have led unambiguously to an increase in aggregate profits.

Notes to Chapter 4

1. The other major qualification is that the assets series is undeflated, so that much of the upward trend is due to inflation.
2. Clearly there were important remaining British companies in particular sectors of electrical engineering, but none with the span of interests possessed by AEI, English Electric or GEC.
3. Of the rest, 4 per cent were vertical — 2 per cent by value — and 14 per cent were diversified — 7 per cent by value (see Gribben, 1974).
4. More than 100 per cent because it appears that internal growth was making a negative contribution. That is, the internal growth of the largest enterprises was lower than that of the smaller. This was even more marked over the period 1930—48, when internal growth appears to have been a powerful deconcentrating force.
5. We would expect the proportion to be smaller because of the merger boom in 1968—9; but there are also technical explanations for the difference.
6. There are of course many problems involved in mapping firms to industries when the firms' output is not confined to the industry in question.
7. Given that the value of CR_{10} in the case of tobacco was already 100 per cent in 1957, there was no chance of an increase!
8. In a symmetric duopoly each firm would have 50 per cent of the market, so that $H = 0.5^2 + 0.5^2 = 0.5$.
9. The relevant information is extracted from Cowling *et al.* (1980).
10. This is a conclusion which can be drawn for Europe as a whole (see for example, various contributions to Jacquemin and de Jong, 1976).
11. There is also the increase in the volume of advertising over time which we have already documented (see Chapter 3). This may be ascribed partly to the creation of tighter oligopolistic market structures via the process of merger, but also to the tendency for advertising to grow over time as private sector output grows, since for a given degree of monopoly we would expect the ratio of advertising to sales revenue to be maintained, so long as the advertising elasticity of demand remained more or less constant. Thus the Dorfman—Steiner (profit-maximising) condition implies

$A/R = \mu\eta_A$, where A is advertising expenditure, R is sales revenue, μ is the degree of monopoly and η_A is the advertising elasticity of demand, i.e. $(\partial X/\partial A)(A/X)$.

12. For the giant firms involved there is often a problem of making adequate comparisons, simply because they often do dominate the industry in question.

13. There is also a question mark about Kamerschen's sample since he appears to have only eight owner-controlled firms in his sample of forty-seven.

14. The problem with this sort of investigation is that it reduces managerialism to simply a struggle between managers and stock-holders, when we need to distinguish at least two basic struggles: that between big capital, internally represented, and small capital, external to the corporation; and that between top management, usually with a major equity holding, and lower levels of manage-ment. McEachern (1975) distinguishes three control groups and reports that where the dominant stockholder has internal access to the flow of pecuniary and non-pecuniary managerial income, the firm grows faster than when the dominant stockholder is not part of management, but that owner-managed and externally controlled firms both resulted in higher profitability than manager-controlled firms.

15. Imagine top management owning 1 per cent of the stock. So long as the utility to them of expenditure out of profits absorbed within the corporation exceeds 1p for every pound, then they would favour such diversion. However, since they may also have control over retention, the incentive to report profits increases since it enables both the firm and managerial utility to grow over time.

16. Cubbin and Leech (1980) conclude, on the basis of a probabilistic voting model, that control can be exercised by a group controlling 1 or 2 per cent of the shares. This would in many cases allow top management to control the corporation from within, e.g. Alfred Sloan controlled about 1 per cent of General Motors stock.

17. The mean profit rate in their sample was 16.9 per cent. Controlling for differences in size between those firms which are 'optimally' organised and those which are not, they report a mean profit rate of 18.26 per cent for the former and 9.58 per cent for the latter.

18. Interestingly changes in capacity utilisation, which would also affect the average rate of profit in the different periods, was allowed for within the equation specification.

5

Class Struggle, the Degree of Monopoly and Distribution

We have argued in earlier chapters that there is an underlying tendency for the share of profits to rise because of the monopolisation of markets but that the actual appearance of a rising share of profits is conditional partly on a distributional struggle between different levels of management and different elements of the capitalist class, and also on the maintenance of aggregate demand, which may itself be importantly affected by managerialism. Until this point we have said little about class struggle between workers and capitalists and its implications for the distributive shares. We now want to ask the question whether or not these processes operating within the monopoly capitalist system are significantly affected by the pressure of workers for higher wages, both directly and indirectly via the social wage. What is meant by union power and is it on the increase? Can a significant redistribution of income and wealth in favour of workers take place despite the monopolisation of markets?

It is sometimes argued that the ability of unions to increase the share of wages depends on the extent to which they can reduce capitalist consumption without endangering the growth of the capital stock, given that if wage share increases at the expense of investment in the short term, then, in the longer term, the level of real wages will be lower than it otherwise might have been (see, for example, Burkitt and Bowers, 1979). Two important qualifications need to be made. First, while the economy is working at less than full capacity, output and income can be expanded and shared between profit and wages. Thus both capital and labour can gain by bringing the economy back to full employment; this was essentially Keynes's view. Wage share could be increased without either a reduction in capitalist consumption or investment. Once full utilisation of capital capacity is reached then of course the underlying conflict re-emerges, but if we regard the existence of excess capacity as the norm in a world of monopoly capital, as we have chosen to do, then it is possible to envisage a higher wage share as a permanent gain from operating the economy closer to its potential output than capitalists would choose to do. Of course this would imply some fundamental changes in the system, but at least we should not lose sight of this aspect of the analysis. The second qualification relates to the level of investment and the rate of growth of income, specifically wage income. It is normally assumed that if worker pressure for higher wages gets in the way of investment, workers will either lose out, in terms of real income and/or jobs, or at least there will be a trade-off between the short-term gains and the long-term losses. This view is predicated on the notion that all investment will contribute, in some way, to raising the real wage and/or the level of employment. Whilst this may be a reasonable approximation to reality in the case of a competitive system, it is certainly not the case in the world we actually face. Profit maximisation in a monopoly world implies investment expenditures designed not simply to raise efficiency or output but also to secure or sustain redistributions in favour of the agent in question. Thus, as discussed in Chapter 2, firms with monopoly positions to protect will logically invest in their defence, and firms seeking monopoly positions will in turn invest in such activity. Similarly, innovations will be favoured which secure and enhance the dominant position of capital *vis-à-vis* workers. Thus if we take a rather more qualitative view of investment we can see that not all of it by any means is necessarily congruent with the long-term interests of workers. This does not mean that workers and trade unions should not recognise that their activities may have an impact on investment and that this may work against their long-term interests. What it does mean is that workers have to involve themselves in the investment decision as well as in pressing for higher money wages if they are to secure their position in the longer term.

We must now specifically locate the struggle between workers and capital in a world of monopoly and assess its significance for capitalist development. There are obviously widely differing views on this subject. Although the neo-classical view on such a broad subject would not normally be articulated, the presumption would have to be that economists working within such a paradigm would regard unionism as either irrelevant to the course of economic development or a matter of second-order importance. Distribution would be determined by the parameters of the production function, assuming as they do that the world is essentially competitive and that it tends to full employment equilibrium. A similar conclusion is arrived at by a strong faction in the marxist camp who conclude that capital accumulation will remain unaffected by class struggle, whereas another faction within the same camp would put class struggle at the centre of their analysis.[1] In terms of the model we have developed in Chapter 2, production workers and the wages paid to them enter as an element of prime costs. This is in contrast to salaried staff, who enter as an element of overhead costs. This distinction is crucial given that so long as the degree of monopoly is maintained, by some combination of concentration, collusion and demand elasticity, then changes in wages, being part of prime costs, will be marked up to preserve the same ratio of price to marginal cost and the share of wages will remain unchanged.[2]

This is not the case with salary increases given that these enter as overhead costs. This will be true whether or not technical or managerial services are provided within the corporation or bought in from outside. In neither case would we regard such costs as varying directly with short-run changes in the rate of output.[3] Thus rising managerialism which may be attributable to the rapid growth of corporations via external acquisition, implying a rising salary bill (with rising salary rates at the top being reflected down the hierarchy to maintain more or less constant differentials), and also increased staffing (expressing the desire by managers to raise the size of the hierarchy and thus their own status and prestige (Simon, 1957)), are both primarily reflected not in prices but in the level of profits, since profit-maximising behaviour will require that the ratio of $(\pi^* + F)/R$ he held constant. Thus if managerialism dictates increased overhead costs then this will, in itself, imply a rising share of national income going to the salariat and a failing share of profits.[4] Even in the long run managers will not allow the rate of output, and therefore price, to be determined by the rewards they allocate themselves since these will be determined by the maximum level of profits which can be extracted from the economy and therefore the decision about output will be determined by profit-maximising policies. Thus our fundamental perspective must be that under monopoly capitalism workers cannot easily raise wage share, while managers can more easily raise their own share of the cake for the basic reason that whereas wage costs are inevitably passed on as price increases, increases in managerial income will not induce such an adjustment.[5] But that cannot be the end of it, since it would seem inconceivable, despite the views of some economists of both orthodox and heterodox persuasion, that class struggle did not matter. What is important is to identify where it matters and why!

Up to this point it might begin to look as if monopoly capital would be indifferent about the 'power' of unions. This would be a misreading of the situation for a variety of reasons. The first and obvious reason is that despite the fact that for any specific monopolist a wage increase could be matched by a price increase, leaving the degree of monopoly unchanged, if this represented a wage increase specific to the firm in question, then such a price increase would be followed by a reduction in sales and a more than proportional reduction in profits, given the existence of overhead costs. If wages throughout the economy rose by the same proportion, then profits would tend to be redistributed through the economy depending on the ratio of imported raw material costs to wage costs in the short run, and in the long run on the degree of substitutability between materials and labour.[6] Thus we can establish that there will be resistance to specific wage claims, even in a monopoly world where wage increases can and will be fully passed on as price increases. Within an oligopoly group, following a similar line of reasoning, Kalecki (1971b) concludes that class struggle will influence the share of wages because wage increases will not be fully offset by price increases. His analysis is really a variant of the kinked demand curve hypothesis which is based on pessimistic expectations on the part of each firm regarding the reaction of rivals to its own price changes. In his model of oligopoly pricing he has the mark-up on costs for a specific firm being conditioned by the level of prices in the oligopoly group, and he argues that the functional relationship with the level of rivals' prices $(\bar{p})$ will itself be determined by trade union activity, i.e.

$$\frac{p_i - mc_i}{p_i} = f(\frac{\bar{p}}{p_i}) \qquad (f > 0)$$

with $f(\ )$ varying inversely with trade union activity. This is neither a very useful description of oligopoly behaviour, since it does not isolate the different ingredients which define the range of possible outcomes under oligopoly, nor a plausible explanation of the impact of worker struggle. We have already isolated the determinants of the degree of monopoly and it is apparent that for the mark-up to be modified would require a change in one or other of those determinants. Kalecki argues that class struggle can have an impact on distribution in the oligopoly case which it cannot have in the case of competition, because if wage increases are specific to a particular firm then price will not increase in proportion, given that it is conditioned by the price of rivals. Thus in a world of plant-by-plant, or more specifically firm-by-firm, union bargaining the degree of monopoly would be lower than it would be if competitive labour markets prevailed. Thus a world of oligopoly with unions would imply a different distribution than one without. In so far as bargaining is firm by firm, and in so far as the spill-over effects from one bargain to another are either unimportant or very much delayed, there may be something in this view. But where bargaining over wages is done collectively for the industry, or where individual firm bargains are rapidly transmitted over the whole industry, then the impact on distribution will be limited.[7] Indeed in tightly organised, concentrated industries we can expect a high degree of collusion over wage fixing as we did over price fixing (see

Chapter 2).[8] This may come about via multi-employer agree-ments or single-employer agreements. In the former case the collusion is overt, whereas in the latter case collusion may be achieved by wage leadership with the dominant firm or firms setting the pace. There has been some dispute about the extent and importance of national wage agreements in the UK and whether or not they are becoming more extensive and important. If national agreements are taken to be multi-employer agreements then obviously we have some measure of the degree of explicit collusion in wage bargaining. Two recent studies, Elliott and Steele (1976) and Thompson, Mulvey and Farbman (1977), reveal that the coverage of national agreements is extensive and rising. Elliott and Steele estimate coverage at 48 per cent in 1950 rising to 65 per cent in 1972, and Thompson, Mulvey and Farbman estimate 62 per cent for 1968 rising to 72 per cent for 1973. This does not of course imply they are particularly important in wage determination, and indeed Brown and Terry (1978) have argued that in terms of their importance for the determination of total wage earnings multi-employer agreements are now in the process of being supplanted by single-employer agree-ments, which are themselves national agreements. Thus following the merger wave of the late 1960s and 1970s there has been a rapid growth in giant, multi-plant firms, and what may have been a multi-employer agreement, or a series of local agreements, has become a single-employer national agreement. Such developments have been encouraged by poorly developed combine committees which have left workers less well organised centrally than locally.

Thus the position appears to be that firms will tend to set up employers associations and adopt multi-employer bargain-ing where collusion might otherwise be difficult, for example where there is a loosely knit, rather large group of employers, but with the monopolisation of markets and the emergence of dominant employers there is no longer any great advantage for the dominant firms to continue such arrangements since they are either internalised in the multi-plant organisation or replaced by the assumption of follower behaviour on the part of the small-scale employers in the same industry.[9] This would suggest that in the case of oligopoly, broadly defined, there will not be any great problem of maintaining the degree of monopoly in the face of union pressures. The institutional arrangements among employers may vary as merger modifies market structures, but employers will tend to offer a co-ordinated front as far as workers are concerned. The main exception to this general conclusion would be during periods of excess demand for labour when such a united front may be inclined to disintegrate.[10] As we have argued before, however, this is not to be regarded as the normal state of the world under monopoly capital, although we may of course observe it at particular conjunctures.

As far as the USA is concerned the evidence indicates that while collective bargaining in the union sector of the economy brought about greater wage increases than would otherwise have obtained, the profit share in this sector was unaffected. Levinson (1954) in fact demonstrated that an estimated five-fold increase in union strength and a three-fold increase in money wage rates over the period 1929–52 was unable to achieve any redistribution from profits to wages. There was evidence of a redistribution away from interest and rent brought about by wage–price inflation but over an extended period such redistributive effects may evaporate. Hines's (1964) introduction of trade union variables into the estima-tion of Phillips curves for the UK over the period 1892–1961 gave pretty robust results indicating a significant link between wage changes and both the change in union membership and its level, but as Pollard (1978) concludes, this only put the steam behind inflation without affecting a redistribution of income as between profits and wages. Our inspection of the evidence of recent history will be postponed until Chapter 7.

It is sometimes argued that workers benefit from the increasing concentration of industry and the creation of giant firms since it will be easier to organise in these larger units. However, we should recognise a two-edged effect (see Levinson, 1967); although union power may increase with concentration, so does the power of capital. Giant firms with strong financial resources and protected from competition are better able to withstand the potential losses associated with strike action. It is also necessary to recognise that the primary determinant of union power in this context is the size of plant and not the size of firm, given that combine committees are in their nature difficult to organise and therefore generally poorly developed. This therefore directs attention to the process of concentration, with merger leading directly to bigger firms without any change in plant size, whereas internal expansion will usually imply bigger plants, given that plant economies of scale exist or are typically increasing over time. This does not of course mean that concentration via merger will not eventually imply bigger plants, but it may delay their arrival when compared with the alternative of internal expansion. The evidence for the UK and the US is certainly consistent with this view (see, for example, Prais, 1976, and Hannah and Kay, 1977). The rapid increase in aggregate and market concentration in terms of enterprises has not been matched by an increase in concentration in terms of plants. The 100 largest enterprises averaged twenty-seven plants in 1958 and seventy-two in 1972, with the average number of employees per plant falling over the same period from 750 to 430. Over roughly the same period, 1957—69, essentially all the increase in aggregate concentration was due to merger and the same was true for most industry groups (see Chapter 4).

Recent results do suggest that wage rates are positively related to plant size and concentration, but that concentration becomes insignificant in the presence of the plant size variable, where plant size is measured by average number employed (see Hood and Rees, 1974). Earlier results for the USA (Weiss, 1966) suggested that the positive relationship between wages and concentration disappeared when the personal characteristics of the worker were introduced, which suggests that concentrated industries were opting for a different type of labour force rather than paying higher rates for a given type of labour. Thus the evidence suggests that perhaps wages are not higher as a *direct* result of concentration,[11] but even if they were this would still be insufficient to conclude that workers collectively would be better off as a result of a more concentrated industrial structure. Not only would wage levels have to rise in those sectors which are being monopolised, but the share of wages in the net output of those sectors must also rise to enable the working class as a whole to extract a larger fraction of aggregate output for its own use. This must be so since if a wage rise in the monopolised sector were met by a price increase, leaving the share of wages in such a sector unchanged, then such an increase would have been achieved at the expense of the real wages of other workers.[12] Thus if monopolisation implies higher wages in monopolised sectors then this implies a redistribution among workers,[13] but in order for a redistribution between capital and labour to be achieved, wage share must increase in the monopolised sector. Obviously our theoretical perspective would suggest that the factors which determine the degree of monopoly will determine the share of wages irrespective of worker pressure; the higher the degree of monopoly the *lower* the wage share. There is as yet no satisfactory published evidence on this question, which is really rather surprising given its central importance. In fact there appears to be only one published article (Moroney and Allen, 1969) and that is less than satisfactory. In it the logarithm of wage share is regressed on the logarithm of the four-firm concentration ratio, and the results are generally insignificant. This is not surprising given the observational technique. Their data comprise nine regional observations on each of sixteen manufacturing industries in the USA and they estimate an inter-regional relationship for each of these industries. This will not be very illuminating because it is unreasonable to assume that *in manufacturing* monopoly power is going to vary regionally in a unified market like the US, and therefore variations in concentration within an industry across regions will not reflect variations in monopoly power — they will simply reflect locational decisions by the major corporations. This is not to say that important regional monopolies do not exist, but they would be in areas such as retailing, services, and a few particular manufactured goods that were perishable or of low value relative to transportation costs.

An unpublished study by Barbee (1974) is of more interest. This comprises an inter-industry estimation for the USA of the relationship between labour's share of value added, concentration and capital intensity. The coefficient on concentration is negative and highly significant for both 1963 and 1967.[14] Unpublished results by Cowling and Molho (1980) for the UK would support this conclusion. In this work the share of operatives' wages in value-added across Minimum List Heading industries (three-digit) in the UK was related to the five-firm concentration ratio and a measure of unionism for each of the years 1968, 1970, 1971, 1972 and 1973.[15] The concentration variable had a consistently negative and significant coefficient but the significance of the unionism variable depended on its precise formulation.[16] Table 5.1 below contains some results from Cowling and Molho. The coverage and duration of stoppages variables were only available in 1973 and, only in the case of the coverage variable,

Table 5.1 *Wage share, concentration and unionism*

Dependent variable: log $[W/(R-M)]$	(1) 1968	(2)	(3) 1973	(4)
constant	−1.180	−0.270	−0.296	−3.720
	(−15.30)	(−1.01)	(−1.26)	(−3.21)
log CR_5	−0.343	−0.220)	−0.231	−0.185
	(−4.89)	(−3.63)	(−3.81)	(−2.45)
log U_1	0.050	0.040	—	—
	(1.95)	(0.99)		
log U_2	—	—	0.036	—
			(1.53)	
log U_3	—	—	—	0.743
				(2.73)
n	106	114	113	85
R^2	0.194	0.106	0.123	0.115
F	12.36	6.59	7.72	5.34

Definition of variables:
W = wage bill (operatives)
R = gross output
M = materials bill
CR_5 = five-firm concentration ratio
U_1 = number of stoppages ÷ employment
U_2 = duration of stoppages ÷ employment
U_3 = coverage of collective bargaining agreements
n = number of MLH (three-digit industries)
t-values in parentheses

Source: Cowling and Molho (1980).

for a restricted sample of industries. Similar equations were run for salary share in 1973 but concentration never appeared to have a significant effect. This would indicate that salary recipients do not lose out as a result of monopolisation, but we may have expected them to gain. Three qualifications need to be made about the results on salary share: (a) the non-pecuniary income of salary recipients is not included and this probably became very important in the 1970s (see Chapters 4 and 7); (b) a variable capturing the degree of managerial control in different industries was not available to be included; and (c) salary recipients may have lost out in the rapid inflation of 1973.[17]

These few estimates of the link between concentration and wage share, if we discount the Moroney and Allen results because of their unsatisfactory observations, point unambiguously to the conclusion that more concentrated industries generate a lower wage share for workers, and there seems some uncertainty as to whether better union organisation or greater militancy can significantly change the outcome.[18] Obviously these conclusions are based on only two investigations, albeit for two countries and for several different years, but there is further evidence that can be brought to bear to support these conclusions. Much work in industrial economics has been concerned with the relationship between profitability and market structure, and in many cases, either for reasons of theory or data, profitability has been taken to be the ratio of a rather gross measure of profits to sales revenue.[19] The formulation suggested by the analysis in Chapter 2 would be the mark-up of price on marginal cost (μ), which in the constant marginal cost case would be equal to the ratio of profits plus overhead costs to sales revenue. Thus for the kth industry the share of gross capitalist income plus salaries in value added equals μ times the ratio of sales revenue to value added

$$\frac{\Pi_k + F_k}{V_k} = \mu_k \frac{R_k}{V_k}$$

We have argued in Chapter 2 that μ_k will be determined by the degree of concentration, the degree of collusion and the industry elasticity of demand. Thus estimates of plausible structure–profitability relationships should give us some insight into the relationship between the degree of concentration and wage share, given that

$$\frac{W_k}{V_k} = 1 - \frac{\pi_k + F_k}{V_k}$$

Generally we might infer a negative relationship between wage share and concentration if we observe a positive and significant relationship between price–cost margins and concentration. However, two qualifications have to be kept in mind. First, all the existing studies of this sort of relationship have deducted the salary bill as well as the wage bill in formulating the numerator. Thus the typical UK study using Census of Production data uses as the numerator of the dependent variable $\pi_k + F_k - S_k$, where S_k is the salary bill, which we take to be an element of overhead costs. If our formulation is correct then this is a mis-specification of the structure–profitability relationship and implies that estimated relationships may appear weaker than they really are. This will be especially true where managerialism is a significant phenomenon, since this will imply that at least an element of potential monopoly profits will be absorbed within the managerial hierarchy and will appear as an enlarged salary bill.[20] If all the extra profits implicit in a higher degree of monopoly were absorbed within the salary bill then there would appear to be no relation between the dependent variable, as traditionally formulated, and the degree of concentration, despite the fact that the wage share (i.e. the share accruing to operatives or production workers) would have gone down.

The second qualification relates to the exogeneity of the ratio of sales revenue to value-added, R_k/V_k. This can be broken down into two components, the degree of monopoly, μ_k, and the ratio of materials expenditure to wage bill, M_k/W_k. Provided M/W is determined exogenously, a positive relationship between μ and concentration will imply a *negative* relationship between wages and concentration. The relationship will still hold, but will be more complicated, if

M/W is positively related to μ. However, if M/W is negatively related to μ then despite the existence of a positive link between concentration and μ this will not necessarily imply a negative relation between concentration and wage share. This would come about if union pressure on monopolised industries led to wage levels which were higher than in more competitive sectors. Workers collectively within a nation state could by this mechanism gain at the expense of foreign workers, but there would be an inevitable adjustment given that such wage increases would be marked up to preserve the appropriate degree of monopoly. At the national level this would eventually imply devaluation or deflation in order to preserve the balance of payments, but at the level of the firm or industry there would be an inducement to substitute materials for labour. This could come about via an existing technology or a new technology induced by the resulting disequilibrium, but perhaps the more important reaction would be a tendency to vertical disintegration by firms or industries which felt threatened by an increasingly militant workforce. This would seem an increasingly popular device for circumventing organised labour. It may take the form of an increasing degree of subcontracting with the competitive fringe of firms in the locality or a move towards sourcing from foreign suppliers, who are themselves faced with a less well-organised workforce. To the extent that certain skills are required and transportation costs are formidable this response will tend to be localised, but these constraints will be seen as a challenge to be met. The current development of microelectronics, with its deskilling of much of the work process and its miniaturisation of circuitry, is a case in point which will facilitate the international transmission of jobs. The current general promotion of the small firm may be another aspect of the response by big business to the increased power of unions within the giant corporations. Increasingly the major corporations will become co-ordinating agencies for large numbers of small production units, each supplying services to the dominant organisation at competitive rates and paying competitive wages. One extreme response could be the handing over of control to the workers at the point of production, with industrial capital withdrawing into finance capital but charging the appropriate rates for the use of capital which will limit the income of workers to competitive wages.

Our general conclusion must be that while workers can make transient gains by forcing through higher wages in monopolised sectors, these cannot easily be sustained because (a) they will lead to price adjustments, and (b) they will lead to adjustments implying an increasing dependence of the monopolised sector on the output of the competitive sector, whether domestic or foreign. We therefore conclude that if a positive link between market structure and price—cost margins can be demonstrated, this is likely to imply an inverse link between concentration and wage share. There is in fact some controversy about the link between price—cost margins and concentration. Much doubt has been expressed in recent years about either the significance of the relationship or its meaning. On the first point the pendulum seemed to swing in favour of the importance of advertising and against the importance of concentration (see, for example, Comanor and Wilson, 1967, for the USA, and Holterman, 1973, for the UK).[21] However, as far as the USA is concerned, Weiss (1971, 1974) concluded, as a result of a meticulous survey of the literature coupled with some significant additional estimation, that there are grounds for believing that a significant, but not very strong, relationship exists between profitability and concentration. The US evidence also suggests a significant relationship between advertising and profitability. As far as the UK is concerned many of the studies have revealed concentration to be insignificant, whereas, in contrast, the advertising variable appears to be generally significant. However, as I have argued elsewhere (see Cowling, 1976), these studies raise fundamental questions concerning the specification of the relationships and the appropriateness of inter-industry, cross-section analysis of this type. Where the estimation is restricted to an appropriate cross-section, for example firms in the UK food industry (see Cowling *et al.*, 1975, chapter 2) or products sold by supermarkets (see Nickell and Metcalf, 1978),[22] both concentration and advertising appeared significant. By focusing on the impact of changes in concentration over time Cowling and Waterson (1976) and Waterson (1980) were able to circumvent the major problem posed by the lack of appropriate estimates of price elasticities of demand and found a significant and positive concentration effect in a broad industry cross-section. Geroski (1981) emphasises the non-linearity of the relationship between price—cost margins and concentration and finds a positive association between the two variables despite the insignificance of the linear specification.

It seems reasonable to conclude on the basis of evidence for both the USA and the UK that there is a significant relationship between concentration and price—cost margins, and thus there is every indication from this source, following our earlier analysis of the links between price—cost margins and wage share, that concentration and wage share are negatively related. It therefore appears that, whether or not unions succeed in raising wage levels in monopolistic industries, and on this point the findings are ambiguous, there is a substantial body of evidence coming out of the empirical literature of industrial organisation that they are failing to raise the share of wages in such sectors.[23]

There remains the issue of the interpretation of the finding of a positive relationship between profitability and concentration. We have interpreted the link up to this point as a market-power relationship, but others have argued that the relationship reflects efficiency (Demsetz, 1973),[24] or luck (Mancke, 1974). Firms get to positions of power because they are most efficient or simply by chance, and not by the deliberate acquisition of monopoly power. Whilst accepting that these are possible explanations, (a) they are not exclusive and (b) they do not imply that power will not be used once acquired, for whatever reason.[25] It can therefore be concluded that a positive relationship between concentration and profitability can be interpreted as a market-power relationship, and its existence implies that the working class has not been able to protect itself, at least directly, from the emergence of concentrated market structures. This evidence supports the more limited evidence on the link between wage share and concentration which reveals an unambiguous negative relationship. Thus we have fairly substantial evidence to suggest that, even in a world of organised labour, we cannot assume that monopolisation will not shift income from worker to capitalist, and it serves to remind us that control over pricing and employment as well as control over wages is required before workers can effectively shift the distribution of income.[26] It is to these issues to which we now turn.

In a world in which workers are pressing for wage increases and where these are passed on as price increases, which in turn leads to increased wage demands, and so on, the rate of inflation may move to a level which is either politically unacceptable or leads to a growing balance of payments deficit in a world where exchange rates are relatively rigid. In either case the policy reaction will be a clamp-down on money supply and/or aggregate demand.[27] Such policies in a world of monopoly will tend to lead to the appearances of excess capacity in the economy rather than bankruptcy.[28] To reflate such an economy will simply accentuate the condition, since real wages cannot rise (with wage increases being marked up) and therefore output will not increase unless public expenditure increases, but in the meantime inflation will immediately return and will tend to accelerate for the same reasons as before. Thus monopoly pricing plus worker struggle is a recipe for stagflation. It can be avoided by accepting the necessity of price control in such a world. Only by controlling the mark-up mechanism can union pressure for wage increases be translated into increased effective demand (except as a very transient phenomenon), which will in turn lead to the elimination of excess capacity.

The alternative solution to the problem, and an immediately rational one from the viewpoint of production workers collectively, would be to bargain directly over a share of the cake. This would put such workers on a par with the salariat in that increases in production labour costs would no longer be treated as justification for price increases. Employment would then be restricted by the willingness of workers to work for the wage, or implicit wage, after the bargain is struck and the total wage bill is determined. An example of this would be the all-or-none contract which specifies the number of employees and the wage rate and therefore the wage bill (see Bronfenbrenner, 1950). Kerr (1957) argues that the employer may be able to escape the implications of such a contract by raising price and thereby restoring the share of profits, but this is precisely what would *not* happen. By their actions workers would be converting themselves into an element of overhead or capacity costs rather than an element of direct or variable costs. Thus for appropriate changes in planned output (that is, output *reductions*) the appropriate definition of marginal cost would be simply materials costs. This assumes that the level of employment specified is equal to the level of employment in the previous period and that there are no significant productivity improvements. However, where planned output is greater than that implied by productivity growth, then the appropriate definition of marginal cost will include production labour costs. This is, however, a trivial point since there is no point in a union bargaining for a level of employment *less* than the planned level as determined by the employer. Thus, for the relevant case, all-or-none bargaining implies a reduction in marginal cost when compared with conventional wage bargaining and therefore implies a reduction in price for a given degree of sustainable monopoly. Thus workers, by such means, would be able to make substantial inroads into profits without employers being able to escape by the increased-price—reduced-employment route. Such bargaining could therefore have radical implications for capital, which probably explains why it is very limited in its actual application. Unions would have to be very powerful and aggressive in order to drive such a bargain, and the circumstances in which such a policy would appear particularly attractive to unions, that is, where wage increases would be followed by job losses in the normal course of events, would be exactly the circumstances where unions would be less than powerful. Thus in relatively competitive markets and in periods of recession or depression unions would not be able to establish such a contract, whereas in the more monopolised sectors and in times of boom they would not feel it necessary to bargain over employment since they would feel secure from any threat of job loss. This is not to say that unions do not strive for both wages and employment, but it is fairly obviously the case that unions find it very difficult to limit redundancies. Neither is it the case that if unions were successful in pursuing such all-or-none contracts they would permanently shift the distribution of income

away from profits since there would be a tendency for investment to move away from sectors in which unions had
successfully eroded profits to other sectors in which profits
had not been eroded.

The development of bargains which specify employment
and wages might be seen as one step along the way to worker
control. If workers inside a firm in which such rules operated
sought to maximise their average income, they would seek to
restrict the level of employment and the firm would look
increasingly like the Vanek (1970) labour-managed variety.
If the advent of worker control merely meant the substitution
of the objective of maximum income per worker within the
enterprise for that of maximum profit then indeed enterprises with monopoly power would appear even more
restrictive in their rate of output, and therefore employment,
than capitalist firms, and thus workers in employment could
secure a higher share of national income at the cost of a
higher level of unemployment — a new version of an old
theme. But such analysis is basically individualistic, as is
neoclassical analysis in general, and would seem quite
inappropriate to the analysis of a world of worker control.[29]
The characteristics of the production function can be expected
to change as the social relations of production change, and
we can expect the objective function of the enterprise to
reflect more closely the interests of society in general rather
than simply the narrow economic interests of the group in
particular when worker control becomes the norm rather
than the exception. This does not imply that the substitution
of worker control at the enterprise level will resolve all the
contradictions implicit in capitalist production and render
the requirement for some degree of central planning no
longer operative, but it does imply that the old assumptions
regarding the behaviour of enterprises are no longer admissable.

But obviously any penetration by workers of the decision-
making and control structure of the enterprise is going to be
fiercely resisted by capitalist interests at the present stage of
capitalist development, so that the worker-controlled enterprise remains very much the exception, and typically founded
on a bankrupt or failing capitalist enterprise, and the all-or-
none sort of contract remains a rarity. However, given a

resurgence of union power and militancy it is not impossible to envisage capital looking on the worker-controlled enterprise as a suitable response to such unfavourable conditions for capitalist production. Thus by converting from industrial to finance capital, capitalists could avoid the increasing conflict in the process of production and retire into a position of supplying capital at arm's length to worker-controlled enterprises. Workers would be left to resolve the problems of production and would compete among themselves, that is among worker-controlled enterprises, for capitalist funds. This might be seen as something akin to the capitalist response to managerialism (see Chapter 4) where the answer was the decentralisation of responsiblity for production coupled with the centralisation of capital allocation decisions, with production divisions being left to compete for capital funds. To create conditions under which the response to worker militancy is analogous to the response to managerialism requires industrial capital to settle for takeover terms which reflect the implicit profitability of the enterprise under worker control. Thus the potential stream of profits gets capitalised into the amount of compensation the capitalist receives, and the worker-controlled enterprise becomes part of a production system which remains dependent on capitalist funding.[30] Thus at an appropriate stage of development of industrial capitalism, with its associated development of worker organisation, we may see an organised withdrawal into finance capital. This could of course be pre-empted by the expropriation of assets by the workers, and indeed this possibility would tend to bring forward the date at which capital would propose, or accede to, worker control without expropriation. Given this perspective it is clear that true worker control cannot come about without expropriation. With agreed compensation workers would be exploited via the market for capital rather than in the process of production, and indeed the share of profits could increase if capitalists, anticipating increased potential efficiency following worker takeover, settled for a valuation which exceeded the market valuation of the capitalist enterprise, a scenario which would be realistic where workers were in a poor bargaining position and also recognised that productivity improvements were possible.

Our general conclusion must therefore be that even when traditional union bargaining for higher wages is replaced by bargaining about both wages and employment, or ultimately by full worker control over the process of production, ultimately the distribution of income will be determined by those who control capital. Thus to have a permanent effect on distribution, workers must take over full control of capital. Anything less than expropriation will mean that any changes in the distributive shares will be essentially transient. This does not mean that changes amounting to less than full expropriation will not be worthwhile, but it does require us to recognise the very limited control over the distributive shares which workers have in a capitalist world. It is hardly necessary to add that expropriation is unlikely to be a politically feasible strategy in the foreseeable future.

If we put these various degrees of extension of worker control on one side, we can examine some of the dynamics of traditional wage bargaining where workers form part of prime costs as far as the employer is concerned; that is, bargaining is about wages and not about wage share. If, under such circumstances, class struggle in, say, the UK, is tending to push up wages, but international competition is making it increasingly difficult to pass on such increases in higher prices, then the degree of monopoly of British capital will have been effectively reduced and the share of profits will tend to fall. This is the Glyn and Sutcliffe (1972) story of British capitalism, but since it has more to do with international competition than with worker militancy it fits more appropriately into the next chapter.[31]

There remains the question of the global depletion of the reserve army of labour following the twenty-five years of uninterrupted and unprecedented economic growth after the Second World War and its implications for the class struggle. Some have maintained (see, for example, Rowthorn, 1980) that by changing the balance of power between labour and capital this development offers at least part of the explanation of the falling share and rate of profit. However, within the terms of our model this is not immediately evident, since an acceleration in the growth of wages, or a deceleration in the growth of productivity, due to growing worker power, will simply lead to the appropriate mark-up on whatever the change in prime costs and an unchanged share of profit. This will be true even in cases where the reserve army is totally depleted so long as there remains some excess capacity in terms of plant and equipment. Thus the exhaustion of the reserve army will not lead directly to an increase in labour's share. There can however be indirect repercussions which may lead to this change in income distribution. As implied earlier, if there is unequal development of class struggle across nation states, partly due to unequal exhaustion of the specific reserve armies, then this in turn will lead, via unequal pressure for wage increases and unequal resistance to innovations (labour saving), to emerging balance of payments disequilibrium and to a profit squeeze in those economies where the pressure is greatest, so long as there is no accomodation movement in exchange rates. This will lead eventually to state intervention to secure a reversal of these trends.[32] More generally, if class struggle intensifies globally, similar pressures will lead to a global tendency to accelerating inflation, which will again lead to political intervention aimed at preventing the system getting out of hand, with its possibly radical social and political consequences. This poses an important contradiction for the capitalist system. Inflation is required to sustain the rate of profit in the face of working-class pressure leading to escalating labour costs, but this either leads to growing international imbalance if these pressures are unequal or to globally accelerating inflation if the pressures are general. In either case state intervention is inevitable and is likely to result in a profits crisis. However, such a crisis, with its obvious short-term costs for the capitalist class, is aimed at disciplining the labour force with the objective of removing at least some of the pressure on wage costs and more immediately at damping down the rate of inflation.

The wage—price inflation, and the potential response to it, has been linked back to the rising confidence and militancy of the working class, and this in turn has been linked to a long period of uninterrupted growth throughout the world's industrialised economies. We must question, however, the real extent of the depletion of the reserve army of labour.

Had the growth of production up to the early 1970s just about exhausted the available labour supplies, and was it this that led to the rising confidence and militancy of the working class, or did this come about despite the fact that labour reserves still remained untapped? Certainly Pollard's (1978) analysis of labour supply in Great Britain since the beginning of the industrial revolution reveals a truly remarkable picture of the tapping of an extremely elastic resource by the dominant social class working by a variety of modes. He describes this process as one of 'inner colonisation' which involved increasing hours of work, increased intensity of work, increased working days via the erosion of weekends and holidays and the increase in the size of the labour force via population growth and participation of women and children. He identifies a watershed at around 1850, up to which point labour supply, in its many dimensions, appeared almost totally elastic. Thereafter things changed: real wages increased and hours of work and intensity of effort declined, possibly due to a rising recognition that output could actually be increased in the long term by such changes and that these benefits could be increasingly intern-alised within the more concentrated industrial structures which were emerging. More recently the situation has obviously been very different as far as the older, industrialised countries are concerned, but two potentially important phenomena need to be recognised. First there has been a rapidly increasing population in third world countries, and capitalist expansion has never really begun to use up these growing reserve armies. The current development of the new, microelectronic-based technology will tend to eliminate some of the restrictions on the switch of manufacturing jobs from the already industrial-ised economies via a process of deskilling of work and miniaturisation of the product. Thus the international trans-mission of jobs will be facilitated and the size of the effective reserve armies will be increased at precisely the same time as the reserve army within the already industrialised economies is being rapidly augmented as a result of capitalist crisis.

The other phenomenon relating to the effective size of the reserve army in the twentieth century is the remarkable extent to which the length of the working week has remained essentially constant since the early 1920s in the advanced capitalist economies in the face of substantial increases in standards of living.[33] This is particularly remarkable when set against the experience of the previous seventy years, when hours of work declined precipitously (see Pollard, 1978). How are we to explain the apparent unwillingness of workers to take part of their increased standard of living as leisure? This is perhaps even more remarkable in the light of all the cross-sectional estimates of the relationship between hours and real wages which suggest negative supply elasticities. The apparent paradox is similar, and indeed related, to the observation of a falling propensity to consume in cross-section but a constancy in time-series. Duesenberry (1967) purported to resolve the paradox by reference to the workings of a demonstration effect, but he failed to identify the mechanism which motivated the effect and which moved it in a particular direction. In the case of both hours of work (and the participation rate of married women) and the propensity to consume, it would seem that the creation of wants via the massive advertising activities of the major corporations, and the associated stream of new and differentiated products, could be interpreted as the underlying mechanism whereby leisure time is not increased, and the rate of consumption tends to be maintained or increased, due to the manipulation of preferences and despite rising real wages. As we have argued in Chapter 3, advertising has a major role in putting off a realisation crisis in a world of monopoly capital by encouraging spending at the expense of saving, but it also has the other major macroeconomic function, that of maintaining the size of the effective reserve army and therefore putting off the possibility of an emerging capitalist crisis due to the exhaustion of the labour reserve.[34] People will not only be encouraged to consume a larger fraction of their income than they might otherwise choose to do, but they will also be encouraged to offer a larger fraction of their time to the generation of income in the pursuit of a higher level of consumption of goods.

Although a seemingly plausible hypothesis, the positive impact of advertising on labour supply has not been investigated previously, but some preliminary results for the USA by Brack and Cowling (1980) can be reported. The period

1919–75 in the USA was investigated, given the availability of data on advertising expenditure. The results using Cochrane–Orcutt least-squares regression are given below (with t-values in parentheses):

$$\log L_{st} = \underset{(130.3)}{3.478} - \underset{(-9.1)}{0.200} \log \left(\tfrac{w}{p}\right)_t + \underset{(7.3)}{0.114} \log A_t$$
$$+ \underset{(12.6)}{0.189} Z_t$$

$$R^2 = 0.912$$
$$DW = 1.75$$

$$\log L_{st} = \underset{(160.8)}{3.474} - \underset{(-12.0)}{0.206} \log \left(\tfrac{w}{p}\right)_t + \underset{(9.7)}{0.041} \log A_t^{K\,(0.33)}$$
$$+ \underset{(-12.0)}{0.220} Z_t$$

$$R^2 = 0.912$$
$$DW = 1.75$$

where L_s is average weekly hours of operatives in manufacturing, w/p is the real wage rate (i.e. wage rate in manufacturing deflated by the consumer price index), A is current real advertising expenditure, $A^{K(0.33)}$ is the advertising stock, depreciation rate is 0.33 – the rate which maximises R^2, and Z is deviations from the trend rate of growth in autonomous expenditure, defined as GNP minus consumption expenditures. It is clear that all the variables are highly significant determinants of the supply of weekly labour hours. The reduction in labour supply induced by a doubling of the real wage rate is entirely mitigated by a trebling in real advertising expenditure,[35] and of course these sort of changes actually occurred over the fifty-seven-year period investigated. The autonomous expenditure variable was included because of the extreme demand conditions characterising the Great Depression and the Second World War. If these years are eliminated from the analysis, an equation without autonomous expenditure performs essentially as well as one with autonomous expenditure.

Thus we have empirical results for the USA which are

consistent with the view that the long-term tendency for the reserve army to dry up because of the increasing unwillingness of people to work long hours when they can sustain their levels of consumption through higher real wages has been substantially offset by the creation of new wants via advertising. Thus not only has advertising tended to switch expenditure patterns and raise the fraction of income which is consumed (see the review of evidence in Chapter 3) but it has served to raise the willingness to work at any given wage rate.[36] For the UK we don't have the same long-run, systematic body of data on aggregate advertising expenditures, nor on hours of work, but the pattern is likely to be much the same as the USA. On hours the fragmentary evidence prior to 1943 suggests a level of fifty-four hours up to the First World War, followed by a roughly constant level of about forty-six hours from 1924 onwards, with some decline in the late 1960s to early 1970s, the only exception being rather longer hours in the war years. This relative constancy in hours over an extended period was, as in the USA, associated with a substantial increase in real wages and, almost certainly, a very substantial increase in real advertising expenditures.[37]

We have to this point examined the implications of class struggle in a world of monopoly where such struggle takes place as a direct confrontation between workers and capitalists, but class struggle can take forms other than simply pressing for higher wages and resisting pressures for higher productivity where this implies a higher pace of work or the displacement of labour. Indeed, since it is difficult, as we have argued, for workers to achieve a bigger share of what is produced by such actions, the success of class struggle is going to be determined by the extent to which workers are able to gain greater control over the capitalist system as a whole. Thus workers operating via the political arena can seek to control prices, subsidise wage goods via the taxation of capitalist income and capital itself, and nationalise without compensation, such actions all contributing to a shift of national income in favour of workers. In addition they can seek increased state expenditure on goods and services, thereby increasing the social wage, which is really a special case of subsidised wage goods. This raises the general question of class conflict in the area of state expenditure and Keynesian policies more broadly defined.

As an antidote to capitalism's tendency to cyclical or secular crisis, Keynesian policies and rising state expenditures may in themselves appear desirable from capital's point of view. The declared aim of full employment may be congruent, at least up to a point, with the realisation of profits and would not in itself be a matter for class conflict, but the form of intervention and its incidence over time would be. Capital would tend to favour tax-cutting policies rather than increased public expenditure, and in this way what may appear as a radical innovation — Keynesianism — may be subverted to the aims of a conservative ideology: cutting income and capital taxes and thus minimising attempts at redistribution, as argued by Stein (1969) and Skidelsky (1977). Thus the 'new economics' of the Kennedy Keynesians in the 1960s ended up by being an essentially tax-cutting policy with its public expenditure plans emasculated. But there are obviously limitations on how far tax cutting can go and what it can achieve, an extreme example being the Great Depression, where tax-cutting policies could achieve very little because of the prevailing low rate of taxation. Class struggle will then centre on the form of public expenditure, with capital pressing for expenditure which will neither compete with private investment nor subsidise unemployment and thereby reduce the will to work of the working class (Kalecki, 1971a). Thus capitalist interests will tend to prefer roads to public transport, and will be against welfare benefits and food subsidies.[38] Military expenditure would seem ideal since it neither competes with private investment nor subsidises leisure.

The other issue, that of the incidence of full-employment policies over time, relates to the broader consequences of such policies. If Keynesian policies convert a system with periodic bouts of heavy unemployment into one in which workers can always expect to find work then the working class will gain in power and confidence to the detriment of capitalist interests. Although 'capitalist crisis' posed real problems for capital it also had a function — that of disciplining the labour force.[39] Its elimination had the immediate effect of raising profitability, but the long-term effect of lowering it. As a result we would expect that at certain points in time full-employment policies would be jettisoned in the longer-term interests of capital, on the assumption that the policies of the state will tend to reflect such interests.[40] Kalecki viewed this process as a political business cycle with its phasing related to the date of elections. But we can also expect a secular tendency away from Keynesian policies as the fruits of a prolonged period of prosperity and the elimination of severe cyclical fluctuations in employment are evident in terms of rising worker confidence and militancy. An understanding of the crisis of the 1970s would seem to require some recognition of this process.

Notes to Chapter 5

1. For discussion of these alternative views see, for example, John Grahl (1979). Union power, along with growing international competition, takes a central place in Glyn and Sutcliffe (1972), whereas for Baran and Sweezy (1966) it has only a minor role. We will look closely at the Glyn and Sutcliffe hypothesis in Chapter 6, where we analyse developments in international trade.
2. This result is conditional on the constancy of the composition of prime costs. Thus if wage increases are not matched by increases in raw material prices then wage share will tend to rise, since the increase in price will be less than the proportionate increase in wages in such cases. In a closed system this qualification does not hold at the aggregate level. However, in an open system wage pressure could achieve at least a transient increase in wage share. It would tend to be transient in so far as it would put pressure on the exchange rate, which would normally imply an increase in the sterling price of imported raw materials, and it would also encourage the substitution of materials for labour in the production process. Thus production methods wasteful in their use of materials but economical in their use of labour would be encouraged. The ratio of wages bill to materials bill would then be conditional on the elasticity of substitution between materials and labour and the relative price movements of these factors. The empirical evidence reported in Chapter 7 shows some cyclical fluctuation in M/W for manufacturing but no observable trend despite a pronounced trend in relative prices. This would suggest an elasticity of substitution of one, implying that the gains from wage pressure would only be transient in this context. Nordhaus and Tobin (1972) provide estimates of the elasticity of substitution between exhaustible resources and a capital/labour composite which tend to be greater than one.

3. Nevertheless this does raise an interesting empirical problem which we have to face in Chapter 7, namely that of disentangling the overhead element from materials costs. Economists normally treat materials costs rather casually, ascribing them all to the direct costs of production. Bought-in overhead labour from *firms* rather than *individuals* (i.e. employees) should clearly not be regarded as an element of short-run marginal cost. Much discretionary expenditure by management would also fall in this category, the rest falling in the investment category.

4. This does not of course imply that managerialism can never play a role in the realisation of profits by sustaining the level of aggregate demand. What we are saying is that *given the rate of output* an increase in managerialism will imply a reduction in reported profits.

5. There is a problem of the dividing line between direct and overhead labour. If we take a broad definition of overhead labour (i.e. a narrow definition of production workers) then we will end up with all types of clerical and technical labour in the overhead category alongside managerial labour.

6. The cost of imported raw materials would include direct and indirect elements and could therefore only be determined within an input—output system for the whole economy.

7. As argued earlier this does not mean that the industry, i.e. the oligopoly group, is indifferent about union pressure; it simply means that union pressure will not automatically bring about an increase in wage share.

8. It should be emphasised that the definition of labour markets will not necessarily coincide with product market definitions, and any mismatch could affect such collusion.

9. Should leadership break down we would expect a move back to a more formal collusive arrangement, i.e. a multi-employer agreement.

10. However, this is precisely the situation in which the assumption of a kinked demand curve implying resistance to price increases would seem least plausible. We would generally expect price flexibility in boom and price rigidity in recession or slump. If wages are relatively rigid in a slump due to union action then real wages can rise with falling food and raw material prices, but wage share will at best remain constant, due to the rigidity of manufacturing prices, or may fall if there is still some downward flexibility in wages. Therefore organised labour, with a kinked oligopoly demand curve in the product market, implies the constancy of wage share rather than its reduction in times of depression. However, as discussed in Chapter 2, there are various ways in which firms can circumvent an apparent kink in their demand curves, e.g. via the adjustment of the quality of their product.

11. A paper published by Geroski, Hamlin and Knight (1980) seems to have unearthed a positive and significant concentration effect in the presence of a size variable. In fact they have not used a measure of plant size but a measure of the size of *firm*. They would

seem therefore to be picking up different aspects of concentration rather than concentration and plant-size effects.

12. Of course in an open economy where monopolisation may improve a country's terms of trade, union pressure could secure an increase in the standard of living of, say, British workers at the expense of the real wages of workers in the rest of the world.

13. If unions are able to enforce higher wages in monopolised sectors then the likely reaction will be an upgrading of the labour force, i.e. firms will seek to recruit, and be able to recruit, a higher 'quality' or more socially acceptable labour force. Thus the positive correlation of wages and concentration will be 'explicable' in terms of the qualitative characteristics of the workforce. These in turn may have either efficiency or discriminatory explanations.

14. The capital intensity variable, although less significant than the concentration variable, is still significant and negative. This result can be explained within a Kaleckian context via a productivity growth differential. Thus a higher capital intensity implying a higher productivity growth, and therefore a faster downward movement in marginal cost, could lead to a higher degree of monopoly, for example with linear demand, an increased degree of collusion (induced by higher overhead costs) or a reduction in the probability of entry.

15. In each year the simple regression of wage share on concentration yielded a highly significant and negative coefficient on concentration. It is thus apparent that union pressure was not able to reverse the direct implication of higher concentration for the share of wages.

16. Alternative measures included estimates of union coverage, union membership and various indicators of strike activity. Obviously strike activity is not simply a measure of union power but a resultant of the conflict between capital and workers. The inclusion of a capital intensity variable did not change the qualitative conclusions regarding concentration or unionism.

17. More recent unpublished work by Cowling and Molho has revealed a strong *positive* relationship between salary share and concentration in 1968.

18. Even if unionism had a significant impact in an inter-industry cross-section it would still not imply that it could significantly effect the evolution of wage share over time at the aggregate level. This would depend on whether the degree of monopoly or the composition of marginal cost was being affected. If the latter, we have already seen that M/W has remained essentially constant throughout the post-war period.

19. This is particularly true of UK investigations, which have relied almost exclusively on Census of Production data which do not identify profit. In the case of the USA there are a number of results where 'profits' are more narrowly defined.

20. Note that salaries comprise only the pecuniary part of managerial

income. The non-pecuniary part will appear either in the materials bill (i.e. will reduce value-added) or as capital expenditures. In so far as elements of the materials bill comprise part of the payment to overhead labour, then materials expenditures are not exclusively part of marginal costs. We might therefore expect M to vary directly with concentration for this reason.

21. Many of the US studies use the rate of return on capital as the dependent variable. Our analysis in Chapter 2 would indicate that this is appropriate where we are examining barriers-to-entry variables but that the appropriate variable for analysing the impact of concentration would be a measure of profit margin. Nevertheless most of the studies have included a capital–output variable on the right-hand side which allows them to be interpreted as profit-margin relationships.

22. The price–cost mark-up was approximated in this case by the difference between the price of nationally advertised brands and the price of own-label brands.

23. Only one study of price–cost margins incorporates a unionisation variable and in this one case it attracts a *positive* coefficient with a rather small t-value (see Cowling and Waterson, 1976), giving no indication of any tendency for unions to eat into price–cost margins. The result is, of course, quite consistent with monopolisation stimulating union growth with the consequent prospect of higher wage levels.

24. Scherer (1980) has argued that much of any apparent 'efficiency' gain is in fact pecuniary in nature, reflecting increased dominance in factor markets.

25. It is also necessary to point out that efficiency is likely to be more closely related to size rather than concentration, and the European experience at least does not support the notion of biggest is best. Samuels and Smyth (1968), Jacquemin and Cardon (1973) and Whittington (1980) have revealed either no relation between the rate of return on capital and firm size or a negative one.

26. This was clearly recognised by Clark Kerr (1957), who concluded that 'only through quite deep penetration into economic decision-making, either directly or indirectly through government, can unionism increase labor's share more than temporarily, that unionism must approach the problem of distributive shares directly and consciously if it is to attain the goal of a higher relative share to labor'.

27. Given that wage increases can be passed on in a world of monopoly, what is it that holds down the level of wage settlement for the industry or firm? The answer is that workers/unions will anticipate that more jobs will be lost the bigger the settlement. The number of jobs lost in the short run will be determined by the degree of monopoly, i.e. by the elasticity of demand for the firms' products given the reactions of rivals. The greater the degree of monopoly, that is the more *inelastic* the demand for output, and therefore

workers, the bigger the wage claim and the higher the wage settlement. But some workers will be displaced if price relatives are disturbed — that is, if the specific union facing a specific industry secures a wage increase higher than the norm. The aversion of workers/unions in the specific industry to such an eventuality will be conditioned by the probability of being rehired, and this in turn will be determined by the (more general) level of unemployment/ vacancies for the type of labour in question. Thus unemployment will moderate wage demands and we would have an inter-industry Phillips curve with the degree of monopoly and the industry rate of unemployment as arguments.

28. This does not preclude the possibility of bankruptcy in such an economy, but it does mean that such bankruptcies will tend to occur in the relatively competitive sectors which cannot easily withstand recession. We are simply arguing that the appearance of excess capacity is quite a normal phenomenon under conditions of monopoly capital.

29. In fact the same individualistic calculus can be amended to reveal that in the short term at least labour management will not be more restrictive. Steinherr and Thisse (1979) amend the objective function of the labour-managed firm to incorporate the risk to the individual worker of being selected for dismissal, which obviously implies that a contraction of the workforce becomes a less attractive proposition for any individual who himself feels threatened. Obviously also, if the worker is to be fully compensated for loss of earnings, then dismissal is no longer attractive for those who remain.

30. It may be significant that GEC, which has been looking around for outlets for its extremely large liquid reserves, has taken a direct interest in the Meriden Motorcycle Co-operative. This could be seen as a tentative movement in the direction of a much more general involvement in worker control. It is interesting to note that GEC was first in the field in the UK in developing a response to managerialism in terms of the multi-divisional organisational form.

31. Rising worker pressure for higher wages is neither necessary nor sufficient to explain a falling share of profits following a rising degree of international competition. For example, exchange-rate policy could serve to preserve the share of profits.

32. A temporary expedient may be found in allowing the exchange rate to depreciate, but with powerful unions this will lead to an acceleration of the rate of inflation and eventually the abandonment of such policies.

33. Over the same period the participation of married women in the market economy has also substantially increased.

34. Note that, as argued in Chapter 2, in these two roles advertising is acting as an antidote to a crisis which may have been partly precipitated by the use of advertising by dominant firms to raise the degree of monopoly and thereby reduce the wage share.

35. Over the period investigated real advertising expenditure actually went up approximately four times and real wages increased by approximately two and a half times.

36. It is likely that this will be reflected in participation rates also, particularly among married women, but we have as yet no evidence on this point.

37. There is systematic evidence over the post-war period with advertising expenditures growing by 20 per cent p.a. over the period 1952–64, clearly implying a substantial increase in real expenditures. Since 1961 estimates of real advertising expenditure have been calculated by the Advertising Association (see *Advertising*, no. 60, Summer 1979) and over the period 1961–78 the rate of growth of real expenditures has averaged 2.7 per cent p.a.

38. It is interesting to reflect on the acceptability of the Common Agricultural Policy in this light. Not to intervene in supporting European peasants could lead to social upheavals which could be inimical to the capitalist interest, but at the same time these same interests would not wish to subsidise food – just the opposite.

39. It may also have performed other functions related to the restructuring of capital via bankruptcies.

40. This is not to say that capitalist interests will be the only ones reflected in the policies of the state. The state is an arena of class conflict in which the interests of both workers and capital are represented – but they have been unequally represented, for a variety of reasons.

6
International Competition and the Rate of Profit

Our central concern with the link between monopoly power and the distribution of income must obviously take account of changes in the degree of international competition. Thus the impact on the degree of monopoly (price—cost margins) of rising domestic concentration could be nullified by growing international competition in both domestic and foreign markets as these markets become more open due either to the removal of restrictions on imports or to declining transportation costs. At first glance it might appear that such developments would lead to an unambiguous reduction in the degree of monopoly and thereby to a reduction in the share of profits. However, there are various objections to such an interpretation. Let us start our examination of this question by considering the generalisation of the degree of monopoly model which was presented in Chapter 2.

Assuming profit-maximising behaviour we derived a statement of oligopoly equilibrium in which the mark-up of price on marginal cost was determined by the Herfindahl index of concentration (H), the apparent degree of collusion (α) and the industry elasticity of demand (η). The apparent degree of collusion is represented by the anticipated reaction of rivals to each oligopolist's output policy, with the value of α determining the position of oligopoly equilibrium between Cournot and full collusion. Provided that the strategy of response to potential entry, whether domestic or foreign, remains the same, then the model requires no further modification provided H and α are correctly measured. This implies that (a) the market shares of importing firms will enter the calculation of H; (b) the market shares of domestic firms will include all the sales of the firm, whether imported or not; and (c) expectations regarding the reactions of importers are embedded in α. Although conceptually this is straightforward, empirically it raises real problems, and we will examine these later. At the conceptual level we still have to confront the question of potential entry where such entry has a foreign base.

In Chapter 2 it was argued that the existence of excess capacity, which could be multi-dimensional, served as a credible deterrent to potential entrants and a strategy of investment in such excess capacity, and therefore in having the potential to increase output would tend to dominate the alternative of maintaining or *actually* increasing output. But what about international competitors — actual and potential? Will excess capacity remain a credible threat and therefore the preferred response, or will firms reduce the degree of monopoly in order to retard entry, and at the limit will all prices be forced to competitive levels by the actuality or prospect of such competition? Various points arise.

First it is necessary to recognise that import diversion could be relatively instantaneous, unlike domestic entry. If this were the case then it would remove some of the advantage provided by excess capacity, since under these conditions it would simply put existing firms on a par with potential (foreign) entrants rather than providing them with an inbuilt superiority. This situation is a possibility when we consider that although world output may be essentially predetermined, the supply to any specific country will tend to be highly elastic. In the case of most consumer goods and sophisticated manufactured products such possibilities would seem rather remote given the complications of complex marketing arrangements and associated long-term contracts, but it may have relevance to some industrial raw materials and simple manufactures. It also remains the case that even if diversions can be rapidly achieved, so long as the domestic structure of distribution, wholesaling and/or retailing remains unaffected then the profits made in that sector will still be determined by its *domestic* monopoly power, and rather than reducing the share of profits in domestic output, the main tendency will simply be to redistribute that profit between the distributive and manufacturing sectors.[1]

The question remains as to whether international, oligopolistic competition generally can be described in this way, with international trade flows reacting smoothly and rapidly to any tendency for domestic prices to get out of line. This would seem improbable as a normal state of affairs for reasons we will elaborate below. This is not to rule out such possibilities entirely but rather to suggest that they should be viewed as transient elements of the international scene reflecting exceptional conjunctures.

First we should extend our earlier analysis of the coexistence under oligopoly of collusion and rivalry. If the response to any attempt to steal a march on rivals is seen by each member of the group to be substantial and immediate then nothing is to be gained and competitive price cutting will not take place. There may be diversion of resources into other activities which imply a less immediate response, such as product innovations, but the point is that the degree of monopoly will not suffer. Potential rivalry, seen more or less symmetrically by all participants, will serve to sustain the degree of collusion. Thus changes on the international scene, such as the creation of a smaller, tighter, international oligopoly group, will serve to sustain the degree of international collusion by increasing the probability that each member will assume retaliation to any proposed aggressive act will be both more likely and swifter. It is also more likely that a common view of the world will emerge which will itself be cemented by the increasing ease of communication as numbers of participants fall. Of course circumstances will change as the balance of international economic power changes, and as a result the degree of monopoly can fall as asymmetries occur which render it profitable for new participants to enter the fray or old participants to take on a more aggressive stance. This will normally arise due to processes of unequal development as between national economies. The emergence of the Japanese car industry as a dominant element in the international trade in cars is a case in point. With the growing strength of the Japanese economy, and substantial protection in their home market, Japanese car firms had a very asymmetric view of rivalry and could see substantial profit opportunities in taking an aggressive stance over market shares. It is interesting to note that when the British car industry talks about the threat of imports and the question of protection it talks not about imports in general, but about Japanese (and East European — but they are not as yet significant) imports in particular, despite the fact that the most buoyant growth in imports is from other countries. We can in fact expect two responses to this sort of asymmetry and the competitive behaviour it leads to. In the short and medium term established, domestic monopolies and oligopolies will seek the help of the state in securing protection, subsidy or restructuring. Again the UK car industry is a case in point, with the state-supported restriction on Japanese imports, the state's direct involvement with British Leyland and its subsidisation of investment and production by foreign car companies in the UK.[2] In the longer term we can expect a further accommodation by US and European car producers to the emergence of the Japanese car industry and the restoration of a more stable, collusive arrangement. The recent agreement between Leyland and Honda is indicative of such accommodation. In some cases of course the emerging power has become the dominant power and the industry has moved back to a similar, or even more monopolised position. The motor cycle industry, dominated now by a few Japanese firms, is an example here.

We have accepted above that changing circumstances can lead to asymmetries which often imply moves away from collusive behaviour, but this need not always be the case. Thus the mutual lowering of tariffs, although changing the environment in which international trade takes place, need not lead to an increase in international competition and a consequent lowering of the degree of monopoly in markets in each participating country. Each member of the international oligopoly will anticipate that any attempt to secure a bigger market share as a consequence of the tariff reduction will lead to an immediate response which will imply that such a move is unprofitable, and thus the degree of monopoly in each country is sustained. This could be a purely tacit arrangement, but more likely it would be reinforced by some more overt action, such as the threat by Courtaulds to enter the markets of potential rivals if suitable agency and franchise arrangements were not concluded subsequent to the creation of the European Free Trade Area (see Monopolies Commission, 1968). Of course, if the lowering of tariffs takes place concurrently with an emerging asymmetry then the degree of competition in some national markets could increase. It is interesting to compare the penetration of imports in the various countries of the EEC. Whilst the UK car industry has been swamped with imports, now running at 60 per cent of the market, in France and Germany the import share remains quite small. In the case of France and Germany there was a symmetry of rivalry which tended to preserve market shares, whilst the UK entered the EEC in a position of weakness, an asymmetry in rivalry — the UK was no threat to the rest of the car industry in the EEC, and thus an aggressive market-share policy could be pursued in the UK by EEC importers, but further analysis must await the later discussion of transnational capital.

However, even where asymmetries appear there are still substantial barriers to entry in a form which would effectively impede any change in the domestic degree of monopoly. Thus although there may be surplus production facilities somewhere in the world economy capable of supplying the UK market, a significant incursion would usually require a substantial long-term investment in assembly and distribution within the UK, often coupled, particularly in the case of consumer goods, with an intensive advertising campaign. Whilst at some point such heavy capital expenditure may be justified, and advertising should be included in the capital goods category, these sorts of considerations do get in the way of the view that international trade flows will smoothly and rapidly accommodate to any domestic price distortions. Rather it would seem that the same considerations will apply to foreign entry as apply to domestic entry, so that the credible threat provided by the excess capacity held by the existing domestic monopoly or oligopoly group will act as a deterrent in both cases.

The discussion to this point presupposes that imported

goods are independent of the domestic monopoly structure
and thus clearly imply an increase in competition in domestic
markets in all cases except for those markets in which there is
no domestic production. This assumption is almost universally
made in the literature, which adjusts the domestic degree of
monopoly for the degree of international 'competition',[3]
and it is almost as universally false. Domestic monopolies
may, and often do, have direct control over the imports in
question. This may come about as a result of the transnational
base of the domestic firm, which allows it to exploit reductions
in tariffs or transportation costs to minimise its production
costs by specialisation in different countries, thereby securing
scale economies, and also to augment its product range
within any particular national market. A good example of
this would be the American car companies operating in
Europe who have responded to the advent of free trade
within Europe with a big increase in intra-company, intra-
European trade. It is interesting to note in this context that
the leading importer into the UK is Ford, which also happens
to be the dominant domestic firm in this market.

If a transnational base did not already exist, the advent of
free trade may induce such a development. Thus the creation
of the European Free Trade Area (EFTA) led to Courtaulds,
the domestic monopoly producer of cellulosic fibres, buying
into European companies which also produced cellulosic
fibre and which had become a threat to Courtaulds' domestic
monopoly following the creation of EFTA (see Monopolies
Commission, 1968). But ownership may not be required for
control over imports. Agency or franchise arrangements can
be concluded, leaving the domestic monopoly in sole control
of the domestic market, or augmenting their dominance of it.
Courtaulds followed this strategy as well and was able to
secure such arrangements more easily by the threat of entry
into the domestic markets of these potential rivals.[4] One can
easily see an accommodation among dominant firms in
different countries being arrived at by a process of threat and
counter-threat, and having as its outcome the maintenance,
or even enhancement, of the domestic degree of monopoly.
Enhancement would come about in so far as smaller and
weaker domestic firms might easily be displaced in the process,

as arrangements are concluded between dominant domestic firms, or as transnational firms are able to strengthen each of their domestic bases. These processes, initiated by the opening up of national markets to foreign trade, will therefore tend, in a world of monopoly, to sustain or strengthen the degree of monopoly. This is an unambiguous gain for the multinational corporation, but in the case of domestic monopolies costs will be incurred as the firm reacts to the increased threat of entry.[5] In terms of our model this would imply $(\Pi^* + F)/Y$ either remaining constant or rising in the face of freer trade, which may imply a rising import share, but at the same time there will be a tendency for F/Y to rise, given that the costs involved would be overheads, which would tend to depress the share of profits. Thus a move to free trade would lead to the increasing dominance of transnational corporations, implying a shift to profits, which in any one country may be concealed by an appropriate set of transfer prices, and increased social inefficiency as domestic monopolies sought to fight off any threat to their position.[6]

There will of course be cases where foreign firms are able to gain an independent footing, and in such instances the domestic degree of monopoly may be reduced, but again there are important qualifying conditions. First we have to be clear that greater competition among, say, manufacturers does not necessarily imply a reduction in the aggregate profit share. The result would only be unambiguous where the distributive sector was competitive. If it is monopolised the greater competition up-stream may simply imply a redistribution of profit between firms, with those in distribution gaining at the expense of those in manufacturing. The other qualification is that the entry of a foreign firm or firms into the market could bring about the demise of the domestic firm or firms, leaving the degree of monopoly unchanged or enhanced.[7]

Thus freer trade and greater imports of goods which are also produced domestically do not necessarily imply a reduction in the average degree of monopoly in any market, and could imply the reverse. However, on the basis of the post-war history of British capitalism Andrew Glyn and Bob Sutcliffe have concluded that British capital has been crushed between the anvil of worker power and the hammer of international competition:

> Our argument in this book is that British capitalism has suffered such a dramatic decline in profitability that it is now literally fighting for survival. This crisis has developed because mounting demands from the working class for a faster growth in living standards has [*sic*] coincided with growing competition between capitalist countries (Glyn and Sutcliffe, 1972, p. 10).

Thus profitability has fallen since higher wages have not resulted in the price increases necessary to maintain profit margins because of rising international competition. This can be accepted as a theoretical possibility, and indeed it has found acceptability across a broad political spectrum, but given our earlier discussion it remains nothing more than that, even if one observes an increasing import share in domestic markets; so we must examine the evidence Glyn and Sutcliffe present to support their hypothesis.[8] Their central piece of evidence comprises a set of regression coefficients obtained from equations purporting to explain changes in wage share for various countries. The basic equation relates changes in wage share to changes in wage rate, labour productivity and world export prices. The sign and significance of the coefficients of the explanatory variables is taken as evidence supporting their hypotheses. However, subject to a reasonable assumption about the relationship between domestic and world export prices, namely that their rates of growth are linearly related — an assumption which is more or less explicit in their hypothesis — these variables form a growth-accounting identity. Thus if W = the wage bill, in this case including salaries, Y = output, p = price level and L = employment, then W/pY is wage share (broadly defined). We can then write wage share as

$$\frac{W}{L} \cdot \frac{L}{Y} \cdot \frac{1}{p} \qquad (6.1)$$

i.e. wage share is the product of the average wage rate (W/L), the reciprocal of labour productivity (L/Y) and the reciprocal of the price level $(1/p)$. Taking logarithms yields:

$$\ln (W/pY) = \ln (W/L) + \ln (L/Y) - \ln p \qquad (6.2)$$

and differentiating with respect to time:

$$\frac{d \ln (W/pY)}{dt} = \frac{d \ln (W/L)}{dt} + \frac{d \ln (L/Y)}{dt} - \frac{d \ln p}{dt} \qquad (6.3)$$

Now assume

$$\frac{d \ln p}{dt} = \alpha + \beta \frac{d \ln p_e}{dt} \qquad (6.4)$$

where p_e is the world export price of manufactures, and substitute (6.4) into (6.3). This yields:

$$\frac{d \ln (W/pY)}{dt} = -\alpha + \frac{d \ln (W/L)}{dt} + \frac{d \ln (L/Y)}{dt} - \beta \frac{d \ln p_e}{dt} \qquad (6.5)$$

Thus, depending on the precise specification, we would expect to observe a significant relationship between changes in wage share and the three 'explanatory' variables *in all cases*, that is irrespective of the behaviour of wage share; it could be rising, constant or falling but we would *always* expect a positive relationship with the average wage rate (holding productivity and the price level constant) and an equal and opposite relationship with productivity (holding wage rate and the price level constant). The point is we cannot use the sign and significance of the coefficients as support for their thesis. Glyn and Sutcliffe also use profit share as an alternative to wage share in some formulations, but since $\pi/(pY) = 1 - W/(pY)$ for their measure of output and profit (π), the equations should be interpreted in similar fashion.

Glyn and Sutcliffe's results are consistent with the above interpretation. Wages and labour productivity are significant determinants of wage share (profit share) with appropriate signs, but this is true for all the OECD countries they examine (for example, the results for the USA are very similar to those of the UK, despite the fact that over the period taken the share of profits in the USA showed no pronounced trend). They also get the same results for different industries:

> We hoped to find that in industries which seemed relatively protected from international competition (e.g. bricks, construction, distribution) wage pressure would be unimportant, whereas in chemicals, engineering and vehicles it would be particularly important due to intense international competition. No such pattern could be distinguished; wage changes generally seem to have had a significant effect (Glyn and Sutcliffe, 1972, p. 243).

Neither did an index of import penetration give the sign they anticipated. They expected profit share to fall as import share increased, i.e. where the growth of import share is added on to equation (6.5), but in fact the coefficient was positive in the profit-share equation.

Despite the above results the authors did not choose to reject their hypothesis — nor should they because they were not effectively testing it. To do so they would need to establish whether or not profit or wage share related to changes in wage costs (incorporating average wage rate and productivity) with the impact increasing over time. The growth in prices would not be included on the right-hand side since it is via the slowing down in the growth of prices relative to the growth of wage costs that profit or wage share is affected. This obviously points to a more direct way of testing the hypothesis, that is via the price-formation equation.

The other piece of evidence offered by Glyn and Sutcliffe to support their view was the apparent decline in the share of profit after the 1967 devaluation. They expected the opposite unless international competition was increasing. But why should we expect the profit share to rise with devaluation? If we assume the elasticity of demand facing the British exporter remains unchanged, then after devaluation the price (in dollars) will fall in line with the fall in marginal cost (in dollars), leaving the mark-up of price on marginal cost unchanged:

$$\frac{P^{\$} - mc^{\$}}{p^{\$}} = -\frac{1}{\eta}$$

Profit share could change for two reasons. First, if devaluation brought a diversion of output to export markets where the relevant elasticities were higher, and therefore degrees of monopoly were lower for British firms, as is generally assumed to be the case, then the profit *share* will tend to fall. But at the same time output increases so that fixed costs per unit of output fall and profit share will tend to rise. The final outcome in terms of profit share is therefore dependent on the devaluation and the accompanying (deflationary) policy package.

We can therefore conclude that Glyn and Sutcliffe offer no satisfactory evidence to support their view that the crisis of British capitalism is due to rising international competition. Neither is it possible to conclude that rising international trade in manufactures implies a falling degree of monopoly within national markets, following the analysis in the earlier part of this chapter. Nevertheless, the Glyn and Sutcliffe hypothesis remains a theoretical possibility, so it is important to sift through the evidence more generally available. First we will extend our model to take account of international competition, and then we will evaluate the cross-sectional and time-series evidence on the degree of monopoly and international competition and offer some interpretation of the results. We will then examine the specific case of the car industry, around which much of the discussion on the impact of international competition often seems to hang.

In a recent paper Lyons (1979a) has extended the Cowling and Waterson (1976) model to incorporate competitive imports and gets the following equation:[9]

$$\frac{\Pi + F}{p^X D} = \frac{H(1 + \lambda + \theta)}{\eta} \frac{X_D}{X_D + M} \tag{6.6}$$

where X_D = domestic output, M = import quantity,

$$\lambda = \frac{\Sigma \lambda_i X_{Di}^2}{\Sigma X_{Di}^2} \, , \, \theta = \frac{\Sigma \theta_i X_{Di}^2}{\Sigma X_{Di}^2} \text{ and } \theta_i = \frac{dM}{dX_{Di}}$$

i.e.

$$\frac{d(X_D + M)}{dX_{Di}} = 1 + \frac{d \sum_{j \neq i} X_{Dj}}{dX_{Di}} + \frac{dM}{dX_D}$$

It is important to note that Lyons is making the assumption that imports are indeed competitive, that is, they are independent of the domestic market structure. If the share of imports controlled by each domestic firm were equal to its share of domestic output, then this formulation would reduce to:

$$\frac{\pi + F}{p(X_D + M)} = \frac{H(1 + \lambda')}{\eta} \tag{6.7}$$

where λ' would now capture the reaction of other domestic firms in terms of either their domestic production and/or their import sourcing. If the biggest domestic firms had control over a bigger share of imports than their share of domestic production, then the appropriate Herfindahl measure of concentration would have a higher value than that defined purely on the basis of domestic output.

If we look at inter-industry estimates of relationships akin to (6.6), we observe mixed results as far as imports are concerned. Khalilzadeh-Shirazi (1974), Dutton (1976), and Hart and Morgan (1977) failed to detect a significant effect of imports on profitability across an array of UK industries, whereas Lyons (1979a) did detect a depressive effect. The studies by Khalilzadeh and Dutton were for 1963 and the sample was limited by data problems, while Hart and Morgan and Lyons were able to use a much fuller sample of three-digit industries for 1968. Lyons's results appear to be replicated for other European countries in the work of Pagoulatos and Sorenson (1976), using data for Belgium, France, Italy, the Netherlands and West Germany, and Neumann *et al.* (1979), but further work for the UK by Rammos (1979) for 1963, 1968 and 1973 fails to reveal a significant depressive effect of imports.[10] Undoubtedly, inadequate data or defective specification could explain the insignificant results, but even if we accept the significant results we are still not able to conclude that the degree of monopoly has been reduced by import competition because of the way profitability has been formulated in these various studies. In no case does the formulation approximate closely to the left-hand side of (6.6). Perhaps the Pagoulatos and Sorenson paper is most interesting in this respect since their dependent variable departs farthest from the specification in (6.6) and yet they get a significant negative impact of import share in four different European countries.[11] The numerator in their dependent variable is valued-added minus the sum of wage and salary bill and depreciation. It therefore effectively excludes overhead costs (F) and this is in no sense a measure of the degree of monopoly which would only require production worker costs to be deducted from value-added. Interestingly Neumann *et al.* experiment with gross profit rates and net profit rates and their results clearly indicate that while the import ratio has a significant negative effect in the case of the net profit rate (i.e. after deducting depreciation), in the case of the gross profit rate the results are less significant, and in the case of their preferred model the import ratio was in fact insignificant. In Lyons's work the essential distinction of his dependent variable from that in (6.6) lies in the exclusion of salaries from F. This is quantitatively quite significant, since by 1968 the ratio of salary bill (administrative, technical and clerical) to wage bill (operatives) in manufacturing had a value of 0.471 (see Table 7.2 in Chapter 7).

In order to be able to understand the empirical results it is necessary to separate out two distinct components in the potential impact of imports on profitability: (a) the possible effect on the degree of monopoly $[(p - mc)/p]$ and (b) the effect on the rate of capacity utilisation. Whilst the first effect is problematic for reasons we have gone into in some depth, the second effect is less ambiguous. Given the level of domestic capacity, and the degree of monopoly, then an increase in the share of imports will inevitably imply a reduction in capacity utilisation. However, if we argue that the degree of monopoly will be maintained because of the control of domestic monopolies over the flow of imports, then why should they acquiesce in a bigger volume of imports? One possible scenario is that they will do this in response to rising domestic wage costs or to the threat of rising wage costs — this theme will be taken up later — but whatever the reason, it can imply the coincidence of a constant or increased degree of monopoly, a higher share of imports and lower profitability because of rising domestic excess capacity. Thus $(\pi + F)/R$ could remain constant but π/R would fall if F/R increased because of falling capacity utilisation due to import penetration. Thus studies like Pagoulatos and Sorensen, Neumann *et al.* and, to a lesser extent, Lyons can come up with results which reveal a depressive effect of import 'competition' on profitability which are quite consistent with the degree of monopoly in domestic markets *not* falling as a result of import penetration. This interpretation obviously requires further investigation, but two pieces of evidence, in addition to the comparisons between gross and net profits in Neumann *et al.*, can be provided in support. First, in Chapter 7 evidence is offered that the average mark-up on marginal cost has increased over the 1960s and early 1970s despite the fact that import penetration grew and capacity utilisation fell. And second, attempts to explain the level of imports of manufactured goods over the 1962—76 period have shown capacity utilisation to have no significant effect in the presence of demand variables (Whitley, 1979). Since this is inherently implausible it would seem likely that the coefficient is being pulled down by the simultaneous existence of a *negative* relationship between capacity utilisation and the level of imports, with the causation going the other way.

For further enlightenment on these issues we turn briefly to examine the history of the car industry in the UK. The behaviour of this industry is both interesting and important. Interesting because the decline in the degree of monopoly (μ) took place before the advent of large-scale imports of cars, and important because about one-third of the variation in the growth of UK industrial production up to the early 1970s was accounted for by the car industry,[12] and since that time there has been a massive increase in import share. Cubbin (1975a) has provided us with a long time series of the esti-

mated mark-up on marginal cost for the domestic car industry.
For 1956—7 he estimates $|(p - mc)/mc| \cdot 100$ to be 35.7 per
cent whereas by 1966—7 it had fallen to 22.9 per cent.[13] As
Cubbin (1975a) points out:

> There can be no unique answer as to why the margin fell.
> Certainly 'international competition' cannot be the answer
> since penetration by foreign firms did not really become
> significant until about 1968.

One obvious explanation lay in the changing degree of excess
demand in the market. The 1940s and 1950s were a period of
full capacity working in the car industry, but by the late
1950s/early 1960s excess demand had disappeared. Despite
this the industry, as Dunnett (1980) argues, embarked on a
programme of rapid expansion in the early 1960s in high
expectations of the opportunities within the EEC. By the
second half of the 1960s the car industry was depressed by
fiscal measures aimed to help sterling, and by 1969 the
industry was operating at 50 per cent of capacity. The
decline in profitability was followed by a decline in investment and as a result the industry was ill-prepared to compete
with imports in the 1970s. The central point is that the initial
decline in profitability was due to the eventual disappearance
of a seller's market in the UK in the post-war period followed
by the creation of substantial excess capacity as a result of
specific fiscal policies. The dynamic implication of this was
the dramatic growth of imports into the UK in the 1970s.
This does not imply that the degree of monopoly has fallen
in the UK as imports have expanded: there is no evidence of
this in recent years. It would appear that the European car
markets are highly cartelised but that the British market
share has fallen with the advent of a wider array of models
offered by rivals. The myth of fierce competition as far as
price is concerned was exploded in an article in *The Economist*
(3 June 1980) which revealed that British prices of British
cars were 50 per cent higher than their levels in Belgium![14] If
we take the Belgian price as a generous estimate of marginal
cost, it can be seen that the degree of monopoly in the UK
car market is very substantial. It is also important to note

that the biggest importer, Ford, is also a leading domestic producer, and that imports by domestic firms have been the major growth element in this market in recent years. When the Society of Motor Manufacturers and Traders or Sir Michael Edwardes (Chairman of British Leyland) talk about the threat of imports, they talk specifically about Japanese (and occasionally East European) imports, and yet the record is clear. Between 1975 and 1979 the share of imports went up from 33 per cent to 50 per cent, but over the same period the share of Japanese cars went up by less than two percentage points (from 9.04 per cent to 10.78 per cent), whereas the share of EEC cars went up almost eighteen percentage points (from 20.34 per cent to 38.20 per cent). In fact the SMMT has taken direct action, with state support, to limit sales of Japanese cars in the UK and yet has at the same time sought to argue against protectionism in general. The answer is clear, the 'British' car industry has an EEC base (Ford, Talbot, GM and even BL) and is not interested in any restrictions on trade and/or investment flows within this theatre of operations. In contrast, Japanese and East European producers are seen as an external threat, against whom Western European and American producers have formed a common front. An increasing accommodation between European and American producers and Japanese producers can be expected in the immediate future. The first signs of such an accommodation are already evident, for example as mentioned earlier in the link-up between BL and Honda.

We can conclude, on the basis of our analysis and the fragments of evidence presented, that freer trade and greater imports of goods which are also produced domestically do not necessarily imply a reduction in the average degree of monopoly in any domestic market.[15] But the argument should not be confined simply to this issue because the general question of free trade opens up wider issues of class struggle and politics. If Glyn and Sutcliffe are right in attributing the crisis of capitalism to growing competition among capitalist countries, then it is difficult to explain the creation of the EEC since this will apparently intensify the competition of capitals. Lest there be any doubt about the view of capitalists regarding this venture there was an almost unanimous verdict in favour of British entry by members of the Confederation of British Industry. Such behaviour is difficult to explain in terms of orthodox analysis of international trade. Whilst the attitude of some firms may be explained by their expectations of direct gains from greater access to European markets, this hardly seems able to handle the unanimity observation. For many domestic industries the benefits of greater access to European markets would be nullified by the impact of greater import competition in the domestic market, if we assume such imports are not controlled by domestic monopolies, and in other cases the balance of advantage could go either way, some domestic industries benefiting from entry and others losing out. If we accept that the expected increase in intra-industry trade was competitive, and that wider economic and political issues remained unaffected, then we might have predicted a split vote among CBI members rather than the unanimous verdict in favour. Thus it would appear more in line with the evidence to regard the EEC as a vehicle for extending the interests of capital via class struggle, both directly and via the political arena.

Given that capital, or at least big capital,[16] is better organised on an international level than is labour, the elimination of national restrictions on trade and the movement of capital will shift the balance of power in favour of capital.[17] Should workers in one country prove recalcitrant then the corporation in question can threaten a switch of production and investment, or with distribution outlets, a switch from domestic to foreign sourcing, and the more unified the international market the more credible the threat. Such threats have been used repeatedly within the UK in recent years.[18]

The existence of a unified international market within which giant international firms are free to operate implies a high degree of capital mobility, which provides a ready mechanism for the processes of de-industrialisation in response to the rise of worker power in the older industrialised economies. Thus in response to rising worker power and militancy in the UK since the Second World War, production and investment will be progressively switched to other locations where the balance of power is more favourable to capital. Within the domestic UK economy this will appear as a rising share of imports, but imports which are controlled by the dominant domestic firms who have made a deliberate choice to move the sourcing of their domestic sales from domestic to foreign production units. The switching of production and investment has in the past been within the older industrialised part of the world, from areas where the balance of power has tipped significantly in favour of labour to other areas where capital has retained its dominance.[19] Increasingly we can expect production and investment to switch out of the older industrialised countries to the previously unindustrialised areas for two basic reasons. First, those segments of the older industrialised areas which have recently seen high rates of capital accumulation will experience growing worker power and militancy as a result, and second, the 'new technology', implying as it does the de-skilling of work, and often the miniaturisation of the product, will more easily facilitate the international transmission of jobs to countries previously ruled out because of their isolation. International patterns of production and accumulation will be constantly revised, but always within the structure of international monopoly capitalism. Capitalism has become increasingly nomadic, leaving a trail of social disruption in its wake. It will be privately efficient for each transnational corporation to adopt such a nomadic existence, reflecting as it does an appropriate response to rising labour costs and the opportunities offered by a more flexible technology, which in turn implies a reduced demand for broadly based skills in the workforce. An international transmission mechanism for production, investment and jobs will have been largely adopted for distributional reasons. Wherever workers act to raise wages or control the intensity or duration of work they will lose their jobs to other groups of less well organised and less militant workers in other countries. Thus de-industrialisation is a consequence of class struggle in such a world. We can expect to see long swings of development and decline being inversely related across economies with different industrial histories — something akin to the alternating long swings of development and decline in the UK and USA in the nineteenth and early twentieth centuries, where movements of population and associated building cycles provided the underlying mechanism. The alternating long swings of international monopoly capital will follow the rise and fall of the power and militancy of the working class. The UK has probably entered a long downswing from which it will emerge, if the monopoly capitalist system remains intact, only as the working class is fully disciplined. As wages fall (relatively or absolutely), and as the intensity of work increases, so the UK will again become interesting for capitalist investment. It is hardly necessary to add that such a system of resource alloca-tion, determined as it is by distributional rather than efficiency objectives, is socially inefficient and involves the wholesale waste of the world's resources. Communities which have been built up to serve the interests of capital will simply be deserted, and plant and equipment will be left idle, not for reasons of efficiency, but because the fraction of output which can be captured by those who own the means of production is too low.

Thus the flexibility provided by a unified international market provides capital with an avenue of control over labour, and as a consequence we can expect to observe capital switch-ing production and investment from country to country in its search for the lower labour costs provided by an unorganised, repressed or demoralised labour force. Obviously one element in this is the political complexion of the state. Thus Brazil, Singapore or South Korea may appear attractive for investment because of the authoritarian regimes they each possess. This may not only imply that wages costs are low, but may also give rise to the expectation that they will remain low even as the demand for labour increases with an increasing rate of capital accumulation. By making investment conditional on the level of wage costs, international firms may be able to gain the co-operation of the state in securing the appropriate general environment in which wage costs will tend to be held down. But there are other ways in which the state can act to make a particular country attractive for investment, and we can expect capital to exploit the potential mobility of capital to secure such action. Thus the rate of profits tax can be bid down by threatening to export investment, and similarly the rate of subsidy for investment can be bid up. Such threats will stimulate competitive profits-tax cutting and competitive subsidisation of investment by national governments, with each government seeking to maximise the rate of investment in its own country.[20] Thus we can expect the advent of freer trade for industrial products and the freer movement of capital to imply a growing share of *after-tax* profits as national governments compete among themselves for jobs provided by monopoly capital. In the case of the EEC this prediction obviously presupposes that either the EEC itself is powerless to prevent the competitive depreciation of the profits-tax base by enforcing appropriate EEC tax levels, or that there is a lack of interest in stopping it by the use of EEC institutions. Currently the position is that the agencies of the EEC are relatively powerless, but neither has there been any revealed propensity to intervene. Without a dramatic change in political arrangements this is likely to remain so.

We may therefore conclude that there is a very real possibility that freer trade in industrial products, and the creation of institutions to facilitate it, can result in a higher domestic rate of profit by increasing the leverage of capital *vis-à-vis* both workers and the state. There can be no expectation that freer trade, leading to greater international competition, will create opposing tendencies except as a consequence of the persistence of an overvalued currency. Assuming either that wage increases will not erode the effect of devaluation, or that devaluation is continuous and in line with the changing disparity between domestic and overseas wage costs, then the rate of profit could be restored by an appropriate change in the exchange rate. This was a matter which was discussed in the previous chapter, and the conclusion reached was that we might expect such adjustment to lead to accelerating inflation and ultimately, and inevitably, state intervention.

Notes to Chapter 6

1. This statement needs some qualification and is discussed in Chapter 2. The key assumption relates to fixed or variable proportions in production. If approximately fixed, then a monopoly at any stage of the chain of production or distribution can extract all the monopoly profits that are available throughout the chain. Substitution possibilities imply a loss of such profits unless all stages are monopolised (see Warren-Boulton, 1974).

2. The general subsidy to Chrysler and the investment subsidy to Ford in South Wales and De Lorean in Northern Ireland are recent cases in point.

3. For example, in the Green Paper, *Review of Monopolies and Mergers Policy* (1978), conventional estimates of concentration were adjusted for both imports and exports, and the adjusted estimates were much smaller than the unadjusted; in some cases the difference is enormous (e.g. for photographic equipment the five-firm concentration ratio goes from 82 per cent to zero!) The estimated differences are entirely due to the incorporation of imports and are entirely predictable because of the way they have been incorporated. The critical assumption made is that imports are not controlled in any way by the top five firms in the industry in question. Thus the adjusted concentration ratio is $R_5/(R + M)$, where R_5 is the output of the top five firms, R is total domestic output and M is value of imports, as compared with the unadjusted ratio R_5/R. Thus the higher the level of imports, the bigger the differences between adjusted and unadjusted ratios. Of course, if the top firms controlled some or all imports then we would have to add some or all imports to the numerator as well as the denominator. The adjusted concentration ratio could in fact be larger than the unadjusted if the share of imports controlled by the top five firms exceeded their share of domestic production. This is by no means unusual (see Cowling, 1978b).

4. Evidence of the effectiveness of Courtaulds' international arrangements was provided by both overseas producers and by UK fibres users (see Monopolies Commission, 1968, p. 123). Overseas producers claimed that fear of retaliation by Courtaulds, in their own home markets or in other export markets of importance to them, prevented them undercutting Courtaulds in the UK. Thus an effective collusive solution is obtained. Fibre users claimed that reductions in EFTA duties had not brought about the expected competition. They claimed that this was due to (a) arrangements made by Courtaulds with Swedish and Austrian producers; (b) the fact that the Norwegian producer supplied wood pulp to Courtaulds and would not compete in the fibre market; and (c) the fact that the Finnish producer agreed not to compete in exchange for know-how from Courtaulds. In the case of Svenska Rayon, where Courtaulds had acquired an interest, prices formerly lower than Courtaulds' were raised as the tariff rate fell. In the case of Lenzing, another company in which Courtaulds had acquired an interest, supplies were withdrawn. It was also claimed that some of Courtaulds' UK customers were unwilling to buy imported fibre for fear that Courtaulds would retaliate by refusing to supply. Two textile companies reported that in times of excess demand they were informed by Courtaulds that any application for remission of import duty on imported fibre would be opposed.

5. This is an example of the social costs arising from attempts by

monopolies to secure or enhance their monopoly positions, or alternatively arising from attempts by other firms to supplant them (see Tullock, 1967; Posner, 1975). The central point is that such 'competition will tend to increase the degree of monopoly rather than reduce it, but the implicit profits will tend to be eroded in the process of competition. With free trade we will tend to get monopoly prices without monopoly profits, an extension of the analysis of Chapter 2.

6. We have discussed the direct response by domestic monopolies of trying to establish control over imports by either buying into foreign firms or concluding arrangements with them — actions prompted by the increased threat of their entry. But the response could alternatively be a political one involving lobbying activities to secure protection. Courtaulds again provide an interesting case. They have been quite open about their attempts to secure a more restrictive import policy for textiles and have linked their acquisition of a dominant position in textiles to the achievement of this aim. Arthur Knight, their former chairman, explains that the acquisition of one-third of the Lancashire textile industry was 'necessary to have any prospect of influencing government attitudes about imports' (see Knight, 1974, p. 49).

7. The motor-cycle industry may be a case in point. Previously it was dominated by a few British firms and now it is dominated by a few Japanese firms, with almost complete displacement of domestic production.

8. It is also necessary to point out that it only remains a strong theoretical contender so long as some sort of fixed exchange rate regime prevails. This was more or less true for the period Glyn and Sutcliffe were analysing, but it became less true in the 1970s. At the present time some people may feel it remains a viable theory even with flexible exchange rates because Britain is now an oil economy with the exchange rate being maintained despite the increasing lack of competitiveness of UK industry. However, this is only happening to the extent that the degree of monopoly and therefore the profitability of the oil sector is growing because of the activities of OPEC. Whether or not the profit share in aggregate will rise or fall as a result depends on the resultant changing composition of British output.

9. Lyons also has a formulation incorporating exports as well as imports, but since this requires the relevant concentration data for export markets which will not be easy to come by, we do not examine its details.

10. These studies and others for the US and a few small economies like the Republic of Ireland, Kenya and Canada are usefully reviewed in Lyons (1979b).

11. Italy was the exception.

12. For the historical importance of the car industry in the growth and fluctuations of industrial production see Rhys (1972).

13. In fact profits (at current prices) were £30 million in 1956 and in 1966, while the number of units sold increased from 1.66 million to 3.08 million!

14. Tax rates were the same in both countries so that does not raise any problems of comparability. Short-term movements in exchange rates could affect the comparisons but they cannot possibly explain the magnitude of the difference. Clearly British (and other European) car producers are operating as discriminating monopolists.

15. It is also relevant to add that of course most goods and services produced, even in a small open economy, are not traded (e.g. 55 per cent of Norwegian output comprises non-traded goods and services).

16. Of course, all fractions of capital are not equally represented in the CBI. Small business is generally underrepresented.

17. This same reasoning explains the aversion of monopoly capital to import controls. Despite the fact that some capitalists could gain in the short term, in the long term controls would imply a shift in the balance of power to labour. Obviously conflicts do arise between different fractions of capital over this issue. There has been a running battle between the small, independent shoe manufacturers and the dominant retailing/manufacturing companies like the British Shoe Corporation regarding controls over imports of foreign shoes. The British Shoe Corporation has been against any form of import control whilst the small independent manufacturers have been conducting a vigorous campaign to get government action to stem the flow of imports. The significant distinction between the adversaries is their control, or lack of it, over the distribution outlets for shoes.

18. Ford (UK) and Ford (Germany) have used similar arguments with their respective workforces.

19. West Germany and Japan have remained favourable to capital accumulation because a very flexible labour supply, due to massive immigration in the case of Germany and migration from agriculture in the case of both countries, has held back the growth of worker power, and because the forces of the left have in both cases been stringently controlled by the state.

20. A recent instance of this has been the competitive bidding for Ford investment by the UK and France.

7
Recent History and Present Crisis

In this chapter the primary focus of attention will be on the behaviour of the profit share and the rate of profit over the post-Second-World-War period in the UK and the USA, from a perspective provided by our previous analysis of the evolution of capitalism in an oligopoly world. Our analysis provides an explanation of the current crisis of capitalism which appears consistent with the evidence, and allows us to identify alternative strategies which will lead to a fuller employment of resources within the existing system, but with the inevitable reappearance of some fundamental contradictions.

The history of the post-war UK economy falls into two phases: the period up to the mid-1960s, characterised by close to full capacity working, with periods of short and limited recession, and the period since, characterised by an emerging trend to rising excess capacity.[1] The underlying momentum of the economy in the earlier period, as with other countries in Western Europe, may be ascribed to the implications of cold war policies, with heavy US involvement in Europe and large-scale rearmament expenditures, the existence of a pent-up demand for consumer goods following the war years, and a process of innovation and diffusion of new technologies largely appropriated from the USA. In contrast with other Western European countries this momentum had fizzled out in the UK by the mid-1960s. The subsequent period was one in which there emerged a pronounced tendency for both the profit share and profit rate before tax to decline. A low point was reached in 1975, with some recovery since, but there is every indication that 1975 levels will be repeated in the early 1980s. Table 7.1 details various estimates of aggregate profit shares and rate of profit.

Column (1) of Table 7.1 reports estimates of the share of real profits in net domestic income (π/Y). There appears to be a mild decline from the mid-1950s, coupled with a certain amount of cyclical fluctuation, but in the second half of the 1960s the profit share appears to settle at an historically low level, showing no propensity to move back up again, and subsequently, in the early 1970s, it drops to a new lower plateau, before falling very steeply to an historic low in 1975.[2] This estimate of profit share should be treated cautiously since it is obviously the product of the share of profits in company sector income and the share of company sector income in total income. If in fact the company sector was declining relative to the total economy, for example due to a widening public sector, then this in itself would tend to produce a declining profit share. This appears to be the case in the 1960s and 1970s, with the company sector share declining gradually during the 1960s and rather more rapidly in the 1970s. The estimates in column (2), which refer to the share of companies' real profit share in companies' value-added (π/Y'), remove this source of bias and show a similar pattern of results. Again there is a significant break in the series in 1966, with profit share moving to a new low plateau before descending even further in the 1970s. The average profit share in column (2) is roughly twice its value in column (1), reflecting an average share of companies' value-added in net domestic income of about 50 per cent.

The question remains as to whether there was in fact a mild decline in the share of profits from the mid-1950s or whether the apparent decline revealed in column (1) simply reflected a decline in the relative size of the company sector. Column (3) reports estimates for the manufacturing sector (π'/Y'') which reveals a fairly constant share in the late 1950s (King and Mairesse, 1978), but unfortunately estimates for earlier years are not available. We conclude that, on the basis of the available evidence, there is little indication of any

Table 7.1 *UK aggregate profit share and rate of profit*

	(1) Π/Y (%)	(2) Π/Y' (%)	(3) Π'/Y''	(4) Π/K
1948	15.0	—	—	—
1949	15.1	—	—	—
1950	14.6	—	—	—
1951	15.4	—	—	—
1952	14.9	—	—	—
1953	15.6	—	—	—
1954	15.8	—	—	—
1955	15.8	—	—	—
1956	14.7	—	21.2	—
1957	14.8	—	21.9	—
1958	14.3	—	22.1	—
1959	14.9	—	22.1	—
1960	15.5	27.4	22.7	14.2
1961	13.7	24.2	19.6	12.3
1962	12.8	22.9	19.1	11.2
1963	13.8	25.0	20.9	12.1
1964	14.2	25.6	21.9	12.5
1965	13.6	24.7	20.9	11.8
1966	12.1	21.7	17.3	10.3
1967	12.0	22.1	18.0	10.6
1968	12.1	22.6	17.3	10.4
1969	12.1	22.6	15.3	10.1
1970	10.6	20.0	12.1	8.7
1971	10.8	20.7	13.3	8.7
1972	10.7	20.8	14.3	8.6
1973	9.5	18.8	10.5	7.2
1974	5.8	11.8	−2.0	4.0
1975	4.7	9.8	−2.0	3.4
1976	5.1	10.7	—	3.6
1977	5.8	12.3	—	4.0

Π/Y real profits (i.e. net of stock appreciation and capital consumption at replacement cost) of industrial and commercial companies divided by net domestic income (i.e. net of stock appreciation and capital consumption at replacement cost). Source: 'Measures of Real Profitability', *Bank of England Quarterly Bulletin*, December 1978. The actual annual data were supplied by the Bank.

Π/Y' share of companies' real profits in companies valued added. Source as for Π/Y.

Π'/Y'' share of real profits in manufacturing (but *excluding* food, drink, and tobacco and metal manufacture). Source: King and Mairesse (1978).

Π/K industrial and commercial companies' pre-tax real rate of return on non-North Sea trading assets: national accounts estimates. Source: as for Π/Y.

significant decline in the share of profits, except for temporary, cyclical fluctuations, before the mid-1960s. The last column in Table 7.1, column (4), reports estimates of the aggregate pre-tax real rate of return on trading assets (π/K) which show the same pattern of behaviour as the estimated profit share in column (3), the low plateau in the period 1966–9, followed by an even lower one in the early 1970s and halving again in the period 1974–7.

Table 7.2 is taken from Williams (1979) and reports real profit rate estimates at a more disaggregated level. A similar pattern is evident in all sectors over the period 1961–77, but some sectors clearly show a much sharper decline in the rate of profit than others. Thus although manufacturing and distribution and services show a similar pattern over time, the profit rate in manufacturing shows a much more drastic decline in 1974–5 than is true for distribution and services. Similarly, within manufacturing, metal manufacture and textiles show a much sharper recession in profit rate in the mid-1970s than do the other sectors of manufacturing. One other difference which stands out is that while wholesale distribution shows a similar rate of return to manufacturing right up to 1974, the rate of return in retail distribution is generally almost double that in manufacturing. This is probably due to difficulties in valuing assets in the case of retailing where land (site location) is important and is only intermittently revalued. It would seem likely therefore that such rates of return are not easily comparable across these very different sectors.

Having examined the evidence on profit share and profit rate, the question to be asked is, what was it that precipitated the decline in the mid-1960s, and what combination of circumstances prevented a subsequent recovery? The proximate explanation for the initial decline in the mid-1960s may be sought in the merger wave of that period which built up to a peak in 1968, with a high level of activity stretching through into the 1970s, and which transformed the industrial structure of the country.[3] This led to a higher degree of monopoly in the UK economy and therefore to a higher ratio of profits plus overhead costs to national income, but for a variety of reasons this did not lead to the emergence of a higher share

Table 7.2 *UK real pre-tax rates of return on total trading assets (per cent)*

	Manufacturing, distribution and services	Manufacturing							Distribution and services[b]		
		Total manufacturing	Food, drink and tobacco	Chemicals and allied industries	Metal manufacture	Engineering, shipbuilding, vehicles and other metal goods	Textiles, leather, clothing and footwear	Other manufacturing[a]	Total distribution and services	Wholesale distribution	Retail distribution
1961	11.4	10.6	11.0	10.3	8.8	10.1	11.1	12.2	13.9	11.0	18.4
1962	10.7	9.7	11.0	9.8	5.9	9.7	9.4	11.4	14.1	10.7	18.7
1963	11.2	10.3	10.4	10.2	5.4	12.1	9.3	11.8	13.8	11.5	17.1
1964	12.2	10.8	11.1	12.0	6.5	9.2	12.2	12.9	13.8	11.2	17.8
1965	11.2	10.2	10.4	11.3	6.4	9.9	11.4	12.2	13.8	11.7	18.3
1966	10.0	8.9	9.8	9.4	4.2	9.1	10.2	10.6	13.2	10.7	17.8
1967	10.4	9.5	10.3	9.1	6.9	9.4	11.0	11.0	13.1	9.7	17.7
1968	10.6	9.7	9.6	11.3	6.6	9.3	10.4	10.6	12.9	10.4	16.5
1969	9.6	8.6	8.8	10.6	4.5	8.1	9.7	8.6	12.3	10.2	14.8
1970	7.7	6.6	8.3	5.8	4.1	6.2	7.2	6.9	11.3	9.9	14.2
1971	8.5	7.0	8.8	5.0	4.5	7.4	6.7	7.3	12.6	9.8	16.4
1972	9.9	8.4	9.9	6.7	4.1	9.1	5.1	9.9	13.8	10.9	20.0
1973	8.1	6.8	7.3	5.0	1.3	7.2	6.5	8.0	11.7	8.0	17.6
1974	3.8	2.7	4.3	3.1	−2.3	1.5	5.0	2.1	7.0	6.3	9.2
1975	3.7	1.9	4.0	2.0	−0.8	2.0	0.5	2.7	7.7	7.4	10.3
1976	5.3	4.3	7.5	4.2	−2.2	5.9	−0.4	4.4	7.9	5.4	10.0
1977	6.6	5.9	6.2	7.7	3.5	6.2	2.9	5.8	7.7	8.1	9.7

[a] Bricks, pottery, glass, cement, etc., furniture, etc., paper, printing, publishing; and other manufacturing industries.

[b] Construction, transport and communication (excluding shipping), wholesale distribution, retail distribution and miscellaneous services.

Source: Williams (1979).

of profits. First the emergence of a greater degree of monopoly, largely as a consequence of horizontal merger,[4] would
immediately imply the existence of excess capacity unless the
profits generated were actually spent. We have argued earlier
(in Chapter 3) that we would not expect an instantaneous
adjustment in terms of investment or capitalist consumption
to the emergence of a greater degree of monopoly, and the
deficiency was not made up by a Labour government following deflationary policies in an attempt to generate a balance
of payments surplus.[5] The emerging excess capacity would
itself tend to reduce the rate of investment and so the realisation crisis would be prolonged. Thus a situation was created
where, although the degree of monopoly had increased, the
implied monopoly profits had not been realised.

We can expect two other tendencies to have also contributed
to the falling share of profits. First, more and more of the
profits generated were being appropriated within the
corporation by the managerial hierarchy. To the extent that
this simply generates expenditure on goods and services (cars,
holiday homes, more opulent offices, more and better lunches,
etc.) then it acts as an antidote to any latent realisation crisis.
To the extent that it involves higher payments to salary
recipients, its aggregate effects depend on the consumption
behaviour (external to the firm) of the salariat. Either way
we can infer that, for any degree of capacity utilisation,
greater managerialism, resulting from the growth of larger
and more complex organisations where control is more difficult, will imply a lower share of reported profits. One
consequence of merger, which is not completely separable
from the one described above, is that costs will tend to rise in
the process of merger as corporations reorganise. These
transition costs, in so far as they are essentially overheads,
will not be marked up and therefore will simply depress
profits for any observed degree of monopoly. These costs
have been widely observed in the literature dealing with
mergers (see, for example, Meeks, 1977; Cowling *et al.*, 1980)
and, because of the massive amount of merger activity in the
late 1960s and early 1970s, they can be expected to show up
in the aggregate measures of profit share over this period.

The other factor which will tend to depress the growth in

the share of profits for any given change in the degree of monopoly over this period is the tendency for overhead costs to increase in importance for technological or control reasons. This tendency may be seen as providing an imperative to the acquisition of increased monopoly power in order to at least maintain the rate of profit, an imperative similar to the Marxian imperative to accumulate under competitive capitalism. Marxian notions of rising organic composition of capital (the substitution of constant for variable capital) would be one variant of this process — the tendency for a rising share of overhead labour, administrative, technical and clerical, would be a further component.[6] Rising overheads will therefore require a rising degree of monopoly to be achieved in order to maintain the rate of profit, assuming the rate of exploitation for a given degree of monopoly remains constant.[7] But a rising degree of monopoly will itself imply rising overheads due to the impact, already discussed, of the emergence of larger and more complex organisations, but also because of the larger amounts of planned excess capacity required to secure such positions of monopoly power from encroachment by rival capitals. Thus a self-sustaining process will tend to emerge with a rising degree of monopoly interacting with rising overheads in an upward spiral.

Within the terms of the model developed, it is apparent that, although $(\pi^* + F)/Y$ is expected to rise as the degree of monopoly rises, this is quite consistent with π/Y falling, the two phenomena being linked by realisation, managerial or technological hypotheses. To begin to distinguish between these alternatives requires data on the average degree of monopoly, the level of excess capacity, the salary share and the non-pecuniary income of management and the capital—output ratio. The other element in the determination of the share of profits is the share of imports. Assuming domestic output and the degree of monopoly are unaffected, rising expenditure on imports implies a rising share of profits, since import costs will be marked up by the domestic monopoly structure and real wages will therefore tend to fall, but in so far as imports replace domestic output they can reduce profit share and profit rate as overhead costs are spread over a reduced domestic output.[8] Thus in the case of imports of manufactured goods the effect might be expected to be a reduction in profit share even if there is no reduction in the degree of monopoly, but in the case of raw materials an increase in their price should raise the share of profits.[9] To determine the implications for profit share we will need to know not only the aggregate import share but also its breakdown into imports of manufactured goods and imports of raw materials.

The above discussion is relevant to the whole period from the mid-1960s on, but obviously the 1970s, and particularly the period since 1973, have witnessed a very different environment for western capital. In 1973 there was a dramatic change in the terms of trade of manufactures *vis-à-vis* raw materials, particularly energy. So long as the degree of monopoly in the markets for manufactures remained unimpaired then the appropriate (profit-maximising) response would have been a price increase for manufactures in line with the increase in marginal cost. Such an adjustment would increase the share of profits within the industrialised countries, and if output was maintained in the total system then profits within the industrial capitalist system would have gone up. At the same time real wages in this part of the world would have fallen and this would ensure that the terms of trade for raw materials' producers would have improved despite the adjustments in the price of manufactures. Thus those controlling the supply of raw materials and those controlling the supply of manufactured goods would have gained at the expense of the working class. Although obviously defective, this scenario is a useful point of departure in assessing the events following 1973. It is clear that the extremely large changes in raw material prices brought about massive dislocations in the world capitalist system. This was perhaps particularly true for the UK, given that the Price Commission was established with quite mechanical rules which implied that increases in costs could not be immediately matched by the price increases which would be required for profit maximisation. The Commission followed different rules in the case of manufacturing and services on the one hand and distribution on the other. Prices in manufacturing and services were controlled via (a) an allowable cost regime, and (b) maximum profit margins, and under (a) only a percentage of labour costs were allowed. In addition, pre-notification of price increases was required and prices could be frozen for up to four months while investigations proceeded. In contrast, for distribution, both wholesale and retail, no reference to cost was made and no pre-notification was required. Regulation was purely via gross and net profit margins. Given these rules it is clear that manufacturing was particularly vulnerable. For distribution the measured degree of monopoly was not allowed to rise, but regulation by margin encourages the growth of costs which provide utility to the controllers of the firm, and the impact on the service sector was minimised by the unimportance of raw material inputs.[10] The profit rates reported in Table 7.2 would appear to reflect the differential impact of the Price Commission on manufacturing and distribution. For example, in 1975 the rate of return in manufacturing was less than one-quarter of its level in 1972, whereas for distribution and services it was more than one-half of its own 1972 level.

It would seem clear therefore that the degree of monopoly in the manufacturing sector was reduced by the activities of the Price Commission, particularly since the period of its operation was one of rapidly rising costs. This leads us to the conclusion that the level of economic activity in the UK over this period was maintained at a higher level than might have been the case in the absence of the Price Commission, given that the reduction in real wages was postponed and therefore the full consequences for the UK of a world realisation crisis provoked by OPEC were temporarily avoided. It should be recalled that so long as the degree of monopoly is not reduced, increases in raw material prices will not reduce profits directly, indeed they will tend to raise profit share. But this is failing to take account of wage bargaining. We would expect unions to fight at least to maintain real wages so that profit share may remain unaffected. However, the actions of OPEC, unless accompanied by an immediate and fully compensating expenditure on investment and/or consumption goods, would imply a global realisation crisis. Such a crisis would have its roots in the initial dramatic increase in the degree of monopoly in a crucial sector of the world economy. The crisis could be mitigated by non-OPEC countries running corresponding deficits and thus maintaining the world level of effective demand. This policy was espoused by the then British Chancellor of the Exchequer, Denis Healey, over the first period of the oil crisis when wages were allowed to increase at a fast rate, but the Price Commission rules interfered with the automatic passing on of such wage increases in the form of price increases. However, in 1976 the rules of the Commission were crucially amended to allow essentially all cost increases to be passed on, subject to profit-margin constraints; in 1977 the Commission was converted to an anti-trust agency with no automatic control over price inflation, and finally in 1979 it was abolished. From our point of view the big change came in 1976, since the change in rules allowed the underlying pricing mechanism to reassert itself — escalating costs could again be passed on provided the degree of monopoly had not been eroded. It was also the case soon after this that the advanced capitalist economies no longer advocated running large deficits in order to compensate for the large surpluses of the OPEC countries. This implied the ending of any pretence to protect the world from a massive realisation crisis precipitated by OPEC.[11]

Having sketched out a particular interpretation of the evolution of the distributive shares and the rate of profit for the UK over the post-war period and particularly since the mid-1960s, it is now necessary to pull together the available evidence to see whether or not the empirical record is consistent with such an interpretation. To come to anything like a definitive conclusion would require a major research programme, but some fragmentary evidence can be pieced together which may be regarded as offering some preliminary support for the particular view of the world which this book has sought to establish. We report below the available evidence for the UK on the evolution over the post-war period of the degree of monopoly, capacity utilisation and salaries and raw materials costs, together with incidental observations on import penetration and capital—output ratios.

The Degree of Monopoly (μ)

Following the discussion in Chapter 2, the degree of monopoly (μ) is defined as the ratio of sales revenue minus wage and materials costs to sales revenue. The Census of Production provides data on these items for both manufacturing and non-manufacturing industry. Non-manufacturing consists essentially of mining, the public utilities, including transportation, and construction, and we have chosen to leave these out of the aggregate measure because they are either nationalised (mining and the public utilities) or perhaps more representative of the competitive sector of the economy (construction).[12] The degree of monopoly has therefore been calculated for all manufacturing industries (in aggregate) for each census year for the period 1948—75 inclusive. This would seem to be the crucial sector to seek to demonstrate that the degree of monopoly has risen over time, given that manufacturing is most vulnerable to international competition. If it can be demonstrated that, despite considerable import penetration, this sector has increased its apparent degree of monopoly, then it would seem plausible to assume that for other less vulnerable sectors where concentration has increased the degree of monopoly will have also increased.

Obviously the average degree of monopoly in manufacturing is affected both by changes in the degree of monopoly within specific manufacturing industries and by changes in the industrial composition of the manufacturing sector. Thus monopolisation can increase either by a relative expansion of monopolised industries or by the increased degree of monopoly of industries in general. The aggregate data capture both these effects, but to illustrate the relative importance of the underlying causes, estimates of changes in the degree of monopoly in some constituent industries where the data are comparable over time are also reported.

In deriving a time-series for μ at either aggregate or disaggregated levels a problem is raised by the possibility of changes in the degree of vertical integration. The Census data are reported at establishment (plant) level so that any increase or decrease over time in the degree of vertical integration at *establishment* level could cloud the true picture. If such vertical integration were increasing over time then this in itself would tend to bias up the estimate of the growth in the degree of monopoly.[13] To assess this possible source of bias a check was made to see if inter-establishment, intra-industry sales had increased over time. Using the 1963 and 1968 input—output tables and aggregating over all manufacturing industries for which comparisons were possible[14] indicated no significant movment in either direction — the ratio of intra-industry (inter-establishment) transactions to gross output, net of such transactions, increased from 8.7 per cent in 1963 to 8.9 per cent in 1968. However, it was apparent that one industry, motor vehicles, dominated the whole calculation. Intra-motor vehicle industry transactions represented nearly 50 per cent of all such transactions for the industries sampled, and had increased significantly over time. Thus while the motor vehicle industry was vertically disintegrating at establishment level, on average the rest of manufacturing industry appeared to be increasing its degree of integration. By deducting intra-industry transactions from the denominator of the estimate of the degree of monopoly, an unbiased series could be obtained,[15] but this is impossible given the lack of data. Instead, in calculating the degree of monopoly for all manufacturing industries, where the bias could be most substantial because of the broad definition of an intra-industry transaction, a measure where all materials costs are deducted from the denominator is also reported. The results, detailed in Table 7.3, give evidence of an aggregate degree of monopoly (column 1) pretty constant during the late 1940s and through the 1950s but starting to rise in the 1960s, reaching a peak in 1972—3 and subsequently falling back somewhat.[16] The alternative measure of μ reveals a similar pattern of behaviour except that it does not finally peak until 1974, which is probably due to the fact that rapidly increasing import costs are getting deducted in the denominator, which may sustain this measure even though the true degree of monopoly is falling.

These results for the aggregate degree of monopoly are in line with our expectations, the upward trend in the 1960s and early 1970s being the result of the very large wave of horizontal mergers over that period, and the fall-back in 1973, 1974 and 1975 being explained by the intervention of the Price Commission. Table 7.3 also contains estimates for a selection of industries for which comparable data were available. These include two broad industrial orders (two-digit

Table 7.3 *The degree of monopoly (μ), UK, 1948–75**

	All manufacturing**		Food, drink and tobacco	Grain milling	Bread and flour	Cocoa choc. and confectionery	Brewing and malting	Electrical engineering	Motor vehicles	Man-made fibres	Weaving of cotton linen and man-made fibres	Footwear	Printing and publishing of newspapers and periodicals	Construction
	(1)	(2)	(3)	(4)	(5)	(6)	(7)	(8)	(9)	(10)	(11)	(12)	(13)	(14)
1948	0.214	0.576	0.136	0.143	0.271	0.222	0.160	0.300	0.172	0.344	0.170	0.231	0.484	–
1949	0.198	0.561	0.127	0.148	0.278	0.209	0.209	0.141	0.292	–	–	0.198	0.453	–
1950	0.201	0.576	–	0.117	–	0.195	–	0.287	–	–	–	0.188	0.424	–
1951	0.193	0.588	0.123	0.105	0.199	0.193	0.151	0.276	0.173	0.371	0.138	0.169	0.405	0.168
1952	–	–	–	0.092	0.182	0.180	0.153	–	–	–	–	0.174	0.344	–
1953	–	–	–	0.103	0.185	0.229	0.168	–	–	–	–	0.181	0.351	–
1954	0.210	0.587	0.136	0.126	0.189	0.244	0.176	0.297	0.188	0.386	0.100	0.200	0.361	0.176
1955	0.204	0.576	–	–	–	0.175	0.180	–	–	0.323	–	0.200	0.359	0.162
1956	0.200	0.568	–	–	–	0.215	0.186	–	–	0.340	–	0.208	0.345	0.153
1957	0.201	0.568	–	–	–	0.221	0.196	–	–	0.340	–	0.200	0.333	0.173
1958	0.210	0.590	0.150	0.167	0.186	0.238	0.206	0.299	0.157	0.296	0.106	0.199	0.340	0.181
1959	–	–	–	–	–	–	–	–	–	–	–	–	–	–
1960	–	–	–	–	–	–	–	–	–	–	–	–	–	–
1961	–	–	–	–	–	–	–	–	–	–	–	–	–	–
1962	–	–	–	–	–	–	–	–	–	–	–	–	–	–
1963	0.246	0.632	0.175	0.193	0.205	0.297	0.238	0.334	0.203	0.409	0.132	0.242	0.399	0.204
1964	–	–	–	–	–	–	–	–	–	–	–	–	–	–
1965	–	–	–	–	–	–	–	–	–	–	–	–	–	–
1966	–	–	–	–	–	–	–	–	–	–	–	–	–	–
1967	–	–	–	–	–	–	–	–	–	–	–	–	–	–
1968	0.259	0.655	0.176	0.214	0.224	0.295	0.219	0.348	0.207	0.373	0.156	0.252	0.424	0.228
1969	–	–	–	–	–	–	–	–	–	–	–	–	–	–
1970	0.251	0.642	0.187	0.244	0.266	0.224	0.242	0.310	0.165	0.334	0.148	0.247	0.440	–
1971	0.269	0.657	0.207	0.288	0.263	0.300	0.233	0.333	0.197	0.311	0.165	0.276	0.489	–
1972	0.283	0.668	0.221	0.224	0.268	0.334	0.253	0.350	0.179	0.303	0.174	0.281	0.492	–
1973	0.281	0.670	0.214	0.203	0.224	0.271	0.281	0.320	0.179	0.371	0.184	0.273	0.480	–
1974	0.271	0.681	0.208	0.195	0.196	0.304	0.241	0.325	0.265	0.316	0.203	0.257	0.445	0.240
1975	0.261	0.657	0.200	0.186	0.232	0.245	0.247	0.330	0.181	0.245	0.190	0.271	0.442	0.250

* For each column all available observations are included.

** In the case of all manufacturing μ is measured either as the ratio of net output $(R - M)$ minus wages bill (operatives) to gross output (R) as in column (1), or alternatively as the ratio of net output minus wages bill (operatives) to net output as in column (2). As explained in Chapter 2, we regard non-operative labour (i.e. administrative, technical and clerical workers) as overhead labour and therefore the associated salary bill is not deducted. In the case of the individual industries the definition is that used in column (1).

Source: *Historical Record of the Census of Production 1907 to 1970*, HMSO, 1979, and subsequent Census Reports.

industries), food, drink and tobacco and electrical engineering, and a series of more narrowly defined industries (Minimum List Heading or three-digit industries) where merger activity has been substantial. Construction is also included as an example of a non-manufacturing industry. In each case the pattern is much the same as for all manufacturing as recorded in column (1).[17] On the basis of this evidence the conclusion must be that the degree of monopoly on average, and over a broad array of industries, has indeed risen over the 1960s and 1970s. The car industry is probably an exception, with the degree of monopoly in the 1970s looking much as it was in the 1950s. Given the considerable excess demand for cars in the early 1950s and the substantial import penetration of the 1970s,[18] it is at first sight remarkable that the degree of monopoly has not declined. It becomes more intelligible when the composition of imports is examined and we assess the considerable degree of control over imports possessed by domestic firms (see the discussion on this point in Chapter 6). As far as the other industries are concerned, some, like grain milling and bread and flour, have not experienced import penetration,[19] but in other cases, like electrical engineering, despite the fact that import penetration has been very rapid, the degree of monopoly has been maintained at a level above what it was in the 1950s.[20] In fact the increase for electrical engineering has not been as large as for manufacturing on average, and certainly not as large as for those industries which do not experience import penetration, but it is necessary to recognise that the monopoly position in such industries has not in fact been eroded, and this is undoubtedly partly due to the degree of control over imports which the domestic monopolies like GEC have been able to achieve.[21]

One other point needs emphasising about our estimates of the degree of monopoly, and that is that the estimates of marginal cost are likely to be considerably overstated and we would expect the degree of overstatement to increase over time, so that the increase in the degree of monopoly over time is likely to be biased down. This comes about because managerialism as reflected in the accounts is not confined to the size of the salary bill but also enters into the determination of the size of payments to other firms for either capital goods or current expenses. In this particular context we are concerned with those components of current expenses which form part of the discretionary expenditure of management — items such as restaurant or executive dining-room expenses, other elements of expense-account living, leasing of cars, petrol, school fees, BUPA, etc. Clearly these should not be regarded as elements of marginal production costs and therefore they should not be deducted from sales revenue in the calculation of the degree of monopoly. Some of these items will undoubtedly have been excluded by the Census definition of 'industrial inputs' which has been used in the derivation of net output,[22] but undoubtedly some elements of overhead, managerial expenditure will remain. We can also expect the relative importance of these elements to grow over time as firms have become larger, and despite the fact that such expenditure could remain small relative to other materials expenses, it will still prove critical in the estimation of μ because these expenses will not be marked up in the pricing mechanism. Further discussion of the magnitude and character of managerialism will be reserved for the section dealing with salaries.

Hazledine (1978) provides an alternative measure of the changing aggregate degree of monopoly for UK industry which shows a similar pattern of results. His measure is the ratio of actual profits to competitive profits (SURP), with competitive profits being defined as the 'normal' rate of return on fixed capital, management (salaries) and inventories times the level of these variables. The 'normal' rate was located by hill-climbing techniques, and the gross rate which maximised the R^2 value turned out to be 0.20. The unweighted mean of SURP for the included MLH (three-digit) industries had the following values:

1954	1.461
1958	1.309
1963	1.596
1968	1.732
1973	1.934

Again from the 1960s on there is evidence of a rising degree of monopoly for the UK industrial economy.

Capacity Utilisation

Capital utilisation is a central variable in our analysis. If monopolisation implies an increase in the mark-up of price on marginal cost, then so long as capital utilisation is maintained true profits will rise, although there may be still a question about who receives them. The possibility that capacity utilisation will fall as monopolisation increases allows the profit rate to fall despite an increase in the degree of monopoly. It is therefore of crucial importance to know whether or not utilisation has fallen over the period in which the degree of monopoly has risen. However, as well as being crucial it is also a tricky variable to pin down, particularly when, as in the case of the UK, there is very little direct evidence. The estimated series reported here assumes a constant incremental capital—output ratio, for which there is substantial supporting evidence,[23] takes 1964(IV) as representing the closest approach to full capacity working, given that this quarter had the largest positive deviation of actual output from the fitted straight line relating average output and capital stock over the period 1955—71, and reveals a declining trend post-1965. With 1964(IV) set at 100, and of course capacity utilisation could have been below 100 per cent in this quarter, the index moves to a low of 80.9 in 1975 and recovers slightly in the later 1970s. If the index is anywhere near correct, then a substantial volume of persistent excess capacity had been created by the mid-1970s — well above anything experienced in the 1950s and early 1960s. But what about the assumption underlying the estimates? Is it reasonable to take 1964 (IV) as a peak and project potential output through to 1978 on the basis of a constant incremental capital—output ratio? One alternative would be to join together local peaks and then interpolate from these — the Wharton School approach. Whilst this would seem perfectly reasonable in the case of regular cycles round a constant output trend, it will fail to detect the impact of a declining output trend on the gap between potential and actual output where there is less than instantaneous adjustment of capital stock to this declining trend. If a constant incremental capital—output ratio is a reasonably accurate description of reality, then the index of capital utilisation reported in Table 7.4 (column 1) provides evidence of such a state of affairs. Some recent estimates using an extended series of observations have come up with alternative peak periods, Savage (1977) with 1969 (II) and Taylor (1978) with 1973. If there is in fact a flattening out over time of the relationship between *actual* output and capital stock then the maximum deviation between the fitted line and the actual observations will tend to appear at a later date — as more observations are added on so the fitted linear relationship will become flatter, and so the maximum deviations will tend to move to the right. This is what appears to have happened. The actual relationship does appear to have flattened out but we have to decide whether this is due to an increased ratio of capital to potential output or to a widening gap between actual and potential output. As we have already reported, the earlier years do reveal a good fit for the linear relationship between output and capital stock (*Bank of England Quarterly Bulletin*, December 1971) and this observation receives support from the *UN Economic Survey of Europe in 1971*, Part 2, which not only indicates constant incremental capital—output ratios in manufacturing for the UK (1950—9, 3.9; 1960—9, 3.8) but also constant (or declining) ratios for most European countries. It also seems pertinent to point out that despite the fact that Taylor takes 1973 to be a year of close to capacity working, the CBI survey for that year reported that 39 per cent of firms were working below capacity.

Given that revising the identity of the peak period as new observations are added is simply a rather crude version of the Wharton School approach, it is interesting to note that large and increasing disparities are observed between Wharton indexes for specific industries and direct estimates of excess capacity in those cases where a declining trend in output growth has been apparent. Taylor, Winter and Pearce (1970) noted that in the case of textiles (1950—67) the Wharton index indicated a much higher utilisation rate than did the proportion of machines in actual use, and in the case of iron and steel (1953—66) and gas, electricity and water (1952—67), whereas official estimates indicated a falling trend of capacity

168   *Monopoly Capitalism*

utilisation, this was not picked up by the Wharton index.[24]
The above arguments and observations would seem to

Table 7.4   *Estimates of capacity utilisation*

	CU (1)	U (2)	V (3)
1948	—	1.6	1.9
1949	—	1.4	1.4
1950	—	1.3	1.2
1951	—	1.0	1.4
1952	—	1.8	1.0
1953	—	1.6	1.0
1954	—	1.3	1.2
1955	98.1	1.0	1.4
1956	94.6	1.0	1.4
1957	93.7	1.4	1.0
1958	90.6	1.9	0.7
1959	93.2	2.0	0.8
1960	98.0	1.5	1.1
1961	95.1	1.4	1.1
1962	92.0	1.8	0.7
1963	93.1	2.2	0.6
1964	98.4	1.6	1.0
1965	98.4	1.3	1.1
1966	96.6	1.4	1.1
1967	93.1	2.2	0.8
1968	94.9	2.3	0.8
1969	94.9	2.3	0.9
1970	92.9	2.5	0.8
1971	89.6	3.2	0.6
1972	89.7	3.6	0.7
1973	91.6	2.6	1.4
1974	85.2	2.6	1.3
1975	80.9	3.9	0.7
1976	84.4	5.3	0.5
1977	84.3	5.8	0.7
1978	83.6	5.8	0.9

CU   capital utilisation, all manufacturing. Sources: *Bank of England Quarterly Bulletin*, December 1971; NIESR *Economic Review*, May 1975; and A. Murfin, private correspondence (estimates for 1973–8).

U   unemployment (per cent of labour force). Sources: London and Cambridge Economic Service (1972) *The British Economy: Key Statistics*, London, Times Newspapers Ltd, and NIESR *Economic Review*, various issues.

V   unfilled vacancies (per cent of labour force). Sources: as for U.

suggest that the index of capital utilisation reported in Table 7.4 is not too wide of the mark. The revealed emerging trend towards a lower level of utilisation in the late 1960s and through the 1970s, in contrast to the earlier essentially cyclical behaviour, is supported by evidence from the labour market. There has been a strong upward trend in the rate of unemployment (U) since 1966, and a downward trend in vacancies (V) over the same period (see Table 7.4).[25]

Salaries, Wages and Material Costs

Table 7.5 reports estimates of the ratio of salary bill (administrative, technical and clerical) to wage bill (operatives) in manufacturing to give some indication of the changing importance of overhead labour. This series provides clear evidence of a rising trend but is likely to be biased downwards over time due to the omission of non-pecuniary payments received by management. Such non-pecuniary managerial income is discussed in Chapter 3, but a recent consultative paper released by the Inland Revenue allows some quantitative assessment of such benefits. The Inland Revenue estimates that between one million and one and a half million company cars escape tax because they are supplied to those earning less than £8,500 (in 1979), the earnings threshold for assessment of such benefits. They predict a tax revenue of £180 million from the removal of the threshold, which implies roughly £600 million p.a. in car benefits to this group, assuming a standard rate of tax of 30 per cent. For managers with pecuniary earnings in excess of £8,500 they indicate a tax yield of £215 million if car benefits were assessed according to Automobile Association scales. The tax rates are higher for this group so let us assume the aggregate benefits are the same as for the lower income group, i.e. £600 million p.a. This implies benefits of more than £1,200 per car, given that the Inland Revenue reveals that roughly a half million company cars are held by managers in this higher income group. The petrol to run this car stock is apparently untaxed, and assuming that used in private motoring is provided free, the benefits for a company car stock at 1979 prices could approximate to £800 million. The Inland Revenue estimates

Table 7.5   *Salaries, wages and materials costs*

	S/W (1)	M/W (2)	P_m/w (3)
1948	0.305	3.98	—
1949	0.309	4.16	—
1950	0.316	4.38	166.9
1951	0.317	4.97	207.6
1952	0.317	4.97	165.8
1953	0.317	4.97	145.7
1954	0.332	4.35	139.1
1955	0.331	4.29	134.2
1956	0.343	4.25	129.2
1957	0.358	4.24	124.2
1958	0.384	4.41	112.9
1959	0.384	4.41	110.9
1960	0.384	4.41	108.7
1961	0.384	4.41	103.3
1962	0.384	4.41	100.5
1963	0.431	4.25	100.0
1964	0.431	4.25	99.5
1965	0.431	4.25	97.3
1966	0.431	4.25	95.5
1967	0.431	4.25	91.4
1968	0.471	4.43	92.7
1969	0.471	4.43	90.7
1970	0.470	4.35	86.0
1971	0.489	4.20	79.8
1972	0.486	4.09	73.3
1973	0.463	4.18	85.9
1974	0.480	4.75	109.2
1975	0.492	4.42	92.0
1976	0.492	4.42	97.5
1977	0.492	4.42	94.4

S/W   salary bill (administrative, technical and clerical)/wage bill (operatives), all manufacturing. Sources: *Historical Record of the Census of Production 1907 to 1970*, HMSO, 1979, and subsequent Census Reports.

M/W   materials bill/wages bill. Sources: as for S/W.

P_m/w the ratio of a price index for materials and fuels used in manufacturing (1963 = 100) to an index of average weekly wage rates for adult males in manufacturing (1963 = 100). Sources: London and Cambridge Economic Service (1972) *The British Economy: Key Statistics*, London, Times Newspapers Ltd, and *Economic Trends*, London, HMSO.

that car and petrol benefits account for about 80 per cent of total fringe benefits, so that the magnitude of such benefits, at 1974 prices, could approximate to £2,500 million.[26] Other than the magnitude of such benefits, the other interesting point about them, as revealed by the consultative document, is that the share of such benefits in managerial income is rising rapidly over time.[27] This is entirely predictable in a time of rapid inflation coupled with incomes policies which are essentially regulating only pecuniary income. Both higher tax bands and incomes policies can be avoided by taking higher income in a non-pecuniary form. Thus our series in Table 7.5 for the ratio of salary bill to wage bill will not only understate the magnitude of overhead labour costs but will increasingly understate them in the late 1960s and throughout the 1970s when there were clear and strong incentives to take increased managerial incomes in a non-salary form.[28] There is in fact very little systematic evidence on managers as a separate category over an extended time series, but the Department of Employment reports that, in the case of engineering, managers comprised 5.9 per cent of the male labour force and by 1972 this had risen to 7.49 per cent. Whilst there is no separate published salary rate for managers, the rate for administrators, technical and clerical workers (male) relative to male manual workers increased very slightly over roughly the same period (1964 : 1.216; 1970 : 1.233). Assuming the same ratio for managers, this would indicate that the share of wage and salary bill received by managers in engineering increased by almost 30 per cent over this period. Given that managerial non-pecuniary income can be expected to have risen faster, total managerial income as a share of total labour income will have increased even faster than this.[29]

Thus we have detected two tendencies operating within the manufacturing sector labour force: a tendency for overhead labour costs (salaries) to increase relative to direct labour costs (wages), and a tendency for managerial labour to increase its share of overhead labour costs.[30] In contrast column (2) in Table 7.5 reveals no obvious trend in the ratio of materials bill to wage bill (M/W), a ratio which enters into the determination of the share of profits. The absence of any clear trend in this ratio for manufacturing contrasts sharply with the dramatic decline in the price of materials relative to the wage rate (P_m/w) which continued from 1951 right through to 1973–4, revealing, as one might expect, a more rapid increase in labour productivity than in materials productivity.[31] On the basis of the evidence any revealed tendency in the share of profits in the UK is not explicable in terms of the changing proportions of materials and labour costs in marginal production costs, although there is clearly some cyclical fluctuation.

The fragmentary evidence which has been pieced together in this chapter may be regarded as offering some support for the view of the world we have sought to establish. We have been able to demonstrate a tendency for the degree of monopoly in the UK to rise from the mid-1960s on, and this has coincided with a tendency for capital utilisation to fall and overhead labour to rise. The outcome has been a tendency for the share of profits and the rate of profit to fall from about 1966 onwards.[32] The history of the US economy has been different in several respects and forms an interesting point of comparison with the evolution of the UK economy. Unlike the industrialised European economies, the US economy operated well below capacity during the 1950s, in the post-Korean war period, and in the early 1960s. Thus our model, which postulates excess capacity as the normal case, has relevance to the US economy over an extended period. No pronounced trend in the share or rate of profit is apparent, especially post-tax.[33] This would seem to be partly due to the fact that the US economy did not fully share in the European momentum of the 1950s and early 1960s, so that there was not the same high level of profit share or rate to decline from. It may also be related to the earlier innovation and diffusion of the most efficient form of internal organisation within US corporations (usually the M-form organisation), which prevented the emergence of a tendency for profits to be increasingly appropriated within the managerial hierarchy.[34] This, of course, does not mean that profits are always realised. Weisskopf (1979), in identifying the components of cyclical change in the rate of profit in the US, concludes that three of the post-war cyclical crises, spanning the period 1954–70,[35] were at least partially explicable in terms of crises of realisation, i.e. part of the decline in the rate of profit was due to a reduction in capacity utilisation. There is no immediate reason why such underlying tendencies should worsen, given that markets within the US have not tended to become more concentrated over the post-war period, most likely due to the outlawing of horizontal merger, although the increasing dominance of the giant firms continues unabated. Equally the US economy clearly has a ready propensity to fall into a realisation crisis without active state intervention aimed at supporting effective demand. This has been the case since 1954, as Weisskopf has demonstrated, whereas for the UK this came more than a decade later, and for the rest of industrialised Europe later still. Now all advanced capitalist economies would appear to be in a similar position, with a recurring tendency to realisation crises. We have analysed earlier the increasing reluctance of governments to raise state expenditure as an antidote to such crises, but it is interesting to observe in the case of the US and UK economies the limited period of their exposure to deliberate Keynesian full-employment policies. The UK followed such policies in the 1950s and early 1960s when they largely served to raise the level of excess demand, generating inflation rather than output, whereas the US economy, which at the same time needed Keynesian policies because of its extended period with substantial excess capacity, received the stern Eisenhower doctrine. In the UK in the late 1960s and 1970s, when expansionary policies to maintain full employment were needed, they were abandoned in the pursuit of discipline. Similarly in the US, following their inauguration in 1964, such policies survived for a mere five years before being abandoned.

Current Crisis and Alternative Strategy

We have established that the historical record for the UK economy since the mid-1960s reveals a rising degree of monopoly, coupled with rising excess capacity and rising overhead costs, partly due to rising managerialism. The period has also witnessed rising militancy by organised workers, which, in the face of rising monopoly, led to an accelerating wage—price spiral, intensified by the dramatic increase in the degree of monopoly in the market for oil, which was eventually damped down by state action. Such action reflected a decisive move away from Keynesian full-employment policies, which in the earlier post-war period had been congruent with the generation of profits, towards policies directly aimed at containing and reducing working-class power. The outcome of this interaction of tendencies has been the increasing de-industrialisation of the UK, incorporating monopoly without monopoly profits, imports without competition (except for jobs) and capacity without production. The process of de-industrialisation has been accelerated by the radical policies of the present administration, the central aim of which is to crush the power and militancy of organised workers by engineering a slump. Not only is the budget deficit not being increased to counter the international tendency for the capitalist system to slide into a deeper depression, it is actually being contracted. Such action, although it will inevitably weaken the position of the unions, will in the meantime bring about a dramatic decline in profitability as capacity utilisation falls. Nor is it very likely that the state has the competence to judge when policies will have to be modified to prevent the whole system spiralling downwards out of control. The question to be asked, given this situation, is, should the left attempt to intervene in the determination of state policy, or should it abstain? Should policies be advocated which may appear to 'save' capitalism, at least temporarily, in order to end the slump and restore full employment, assuming there are such policies available, or should the left remain outside of this, proclaiming the faults of the system and putting forward a programme for undiluted socialism, to be rolled out at some unspecified date in the future when capitalism has finally collapsed? It would seem that the basic question is, would the left be strengthened more by restoring full employment and exposing the requirement of increased profitability for further growth under capitalism, or by allowing capitalism to sink further under its own contradictions. Clearly the latter alternative is very risky, with a move to an authoritarian, right-wing 'solution' being a real possibility, so that it would seem important at least to consider the possible attributes of an alternative strategy within the context of a monopoly capitalist system.

Since the system is operating well below capacity, the first aim of such a strategy would be to raise effective demand by increasing the budget deficit. Without going into details, a package of increased state expenditure, and possibly tax cuts, favouring low income groups with a high marginal propensity to consume, would be favoured. Given more or less constant marginal cost curves up to near capacity working, output could easily be increased, unemployment would fall as more production workers were taken on, and profits would rise as overheads were spread over a bigger output. If nothing else were done then the system would quickly return to an accelerating wage—price spiral as workers tried to increase real wages by pushing up money wages, and, in turn, monopoly capital responded by raising prices. To prevent this happening, and as a beginning to taking over more control from capital, a permanent system of price controls would be instituted. As we have argued in Chapter 5, attempting to make fundamental changes in the distribution of income simply via unco-ordinated wage militancy is a very inefficient way of doing things. To make a substantial and permanent impact, control over pricing and investment has to be wrested from the hands of capital. Whether or not wage controls are needed in addition to price controls is arguable. In a fully adjusted system workers would recognise a clear limit to wage bargaining imposed by the inflexibility of prices due to external control and would modify their behaviour accordingly. However during the transitional period it is likely that lack of experience, confidence or information could lead to unanticipated bankruptcies and unemployment if there were no wage control system. It will also be necessary to begin to modify wage differentials for equity reasons. The introduction of such external wage controls does not mean there is no role for shop-floor organisation. As Burkitt and Bowers (1979) have pointed out, more of the energies of shop stewards could be directed towards extended control by workers over the work environment, including such things as the pace and pressure of work and health and safety aspects.

The other central feature of an alternative strategy advocated by many different groups has been import controls. With comprehensive price controls the requirement for import controls will be reduced, but will still probably remain, especially given the fact that the existence of British oil is serving to maintain the sterling exchange rate above the level at which British manufactures can compete on world markets. Thus to restore full employment, given that the substitution of oil for manufactures effectively reduces employment, will probably require import controls and/or an imposed depreciation of sterling.

Given such a set of policies the economy could be expected to expand to full capacity working over a period of two or three years. Such an expansion would be accompanied by substantial and increasing pressure for the removal of price controls. This would have to be strongly resisted and the permanency of price controls re-emphasised. Given that a fundamental redistribution of income and wealth was being sought, then ultimately there would be an investment strike. Whilst capital would be happy to expand production up to the level of current capacity, the subsequent decision to invest in additional capacity would be conditional on the rate of return at full capacity, which would in turn be determined by the degree of monopoly and the magnitude of overhead costs. If price controls were operated to ensure a reduced effective degree of monopoly then the profit rate would fall and so would investment. Conditions could be created in which capital could be induced to invest at lower rates of profit, for example by reducing real rates of interest, and indeed by controlling capital outflows from the country, but it would also be important to create institutions to allow the progressive socialisation of capital. Private investment would be progressively replaced by state/worker investment, with the state providing money for the setting up of new industries and the revival of others, backing groups of workers or new initiatives. These ventures must be divorced from the old capitalist hierarchy and must develop a new breed of worker-managers. Sectors would be progressively taken over by new public ventures, and not by taking over the more decrepit elements of private enterprise at inflated prices, which is (with some exceptions) the history of nationalisation in the UK. The existing nationalised industries, which of course would also be subject to permanent price controls, would be opened up and democratised, and the whole system would be operated with a judicious mixture of central planning and decentralised worker control, hopefully without either anarchy or massive bureaucracy. Such a programme of gradual extension of control by people over their working lives would seem preferable to simply standing back and waiting for some ultimate collapse of the capitalist system with all the untold suffering it would imply for the great mass of people.

Notes to Chapter 7

1. The degree of capacity utilisation throughout the post-war period is detailed in Table 7.4. Although there are fluctuations, the 1970s clearly remain a decade with very substantial levels of excess capacity. The estimate for 1975, an extreme year, was almost 20 per cent, but current projections for the immediate future look even worse.
2. According to the estimates in Clark and Williams (1978) the previous low in 1931 revealed a profit share roughly twice the level of that in 1975. However, this should not be taken too seriously because of changes in the relative size of the company sector between the two dates.
3. For a detailed account see Chapter 4.
4. Eighty per cent of mergers were horizontal, i.e. between corporations operating in the same or related markets (see Chapter 4).
5. Dunnett (1980) has argued that investment in the car industry in the late 1960s was held back by government fiscal measures, and as a result the domestic manufacturing side of the industry was left in an extremely exposed position in the 1970s. More generally it seems likely that domestic investment was held back by the international role adopted by British capital, which was partly determined by its history but also by the rising power and militancy of the British working class. GEC is an interesting case. Following its creation in 1968 it amassed huge profits which it retained in a highly liquid form whilst prospecting for foreign investment outlets (see Chapter 4).
6. As organisations become bigger and more complex there is a generally observed tendency for the share of overhead labour in total labour to rise (see Cowling *et al.*, 1968). Whilst some of this is undoubtedly explicable in terms of the various facets of managerialism, it seems likely that technological and control factors are also relevant. Bigger organisations will generally require bigger administrative hierarchies and will also imply substitution of direct production workers by overhead technical workers as production units

become bigger, more complex and more capital intensive. With the increasing application of science to industrial production we can also expect a tendency for direct production workers to be displaced by technical workers.

7. Until very recently it would have appeared improbable that the rate of profit could be maintained by raising the rate of exploitation within the labour process, at least in the case of advanced capitalist economies. This assumption must now be open to question with the current attack on the working class.

8. Rising imports can of course imply a falling degree of monopoly, although even in the case of 'competitive' imports this need not turn out to be the case given that domestic monopolies may have control, directly or indirectly, over such imports. For further discussion see Chapter 6.

9. With transnational corporations transfer pricing allows profits to be distributed internationally in some optimal fashion as far as the firm is concerned. This obviously raises real problems in measuring profits for any national economy. For example, at the time of the Chrysler crisis of 1976, the *reported* profitability of Chrysler (UK) may have been well below its *true* profitability (in order to maximise the subsidy the UK government was to give to Chrysler). This distortion could have been achieved by routing the paper transactions covering the big Iran contract via an office in Switzerland and subsequently attributing the profits accruing from the contract to the office in Switzerland by a judicious selection of prices for the CKD ('completely knocked down') vehicles leaving the UK and arriving in Iran, via Swizterland.

10. Although raw materials cost increases were allowed their high rate of increase could restrict profits in two ways. First because prices could be frozen for four months and second because increases in wages costs were only partly allowed. With rapid cost inflation, as in the mid-1970s the temporary price freeze could have a very big impact on profits and the rapid increase in food and energy prices in this period were largely instrumental in raising the rate of wage inflation to extremely high levels.

11. This view is reflected in the current monetarist stance of these countries and the international agencies like the IMF which they dominate. The international recession of the late 1970s, early 1980s, has clearly been engineered by the governments of the advanced capitalist economies, ostensibly to get a grip on an accelerating rate of inflation. Clearly profit rates will fall with the current drastic reductions in capacity utilisation.

12. The point about the construction industry being competitive is arguable. It can be argued that sections at least of the industry have become increasingly dominated by a small group of giant firms despite the fact that the aggregate concentration figures are quite low. With this in mind the estimated degree of monopoly series is reported separately for construction.

13. Imagine two establishments, vertically linked before integration. Establishment A has a degree of monopoly, $\mu_A = (R_A - M_A^1 - M_A^2 - W_A)/R_A$, and establishment B, $\mu_B = (R_B - M_B^2 - W_B)/R_B$, and $R_B = M_A^1$. Then the estimated *aggregate* degree of monopoly is $(R_A + R_B - M_A^1 - M_A^2 - M_B^2 - W_B)/(R_A + R_B)$ which can be written $(R_A - M^2 - W)/(R_A + R_B)$. After integration this becomes $(R_A - M^2 - W)/R_A$, i.e. the estimated aggregate degree of monopoly has increased.

14. It was not possible to compare the 1954 and 1963 input—output tables because the level of aggregation was different, and this would itself affect the magnitude of the estimate of intra-industry trade.

15. The estimate of the aggregate degree of monopoly would then be $(R_A - M^2 - W)/(R_A + R_B - M_A^1)$, but since $M_A^1 = R_B$, μ is $(R_A - M^2 - W)/R_A$, which is the same before or after integration (see note 13).

16. 1975 was the last available year for the Census data when the calculations were made.

17. There are one or two odd results for 1948—9: for example, grain milling, bread and flour, weaving, printing and publishing of newspapers had a very high degree of monopoly in these early post-war years relative to the position in the 1950s. It raises the question as to whether post-war controls on these industries allowed them to secure high prices for their products.

18. In 1968 imports comprised less than 5 per cent of domestic sales, but by 1974 the share of imports had risen to 27 per cent (data supplied by John Beath).

19. John Beath's data for cereal processing indicate an import share of roughly 3 per cent for the whole period up to 1973 when it increased to about 5 per cent.

20. From a low of 1.4 per cent in 1954, the share of imports in electrical engineering grew to 11.4 per cent in 1968, and subsequently to 31.5 per cent in 1974 (John Beath's data).

21. For a detailed account of the activities of GEC see Dutton (1980).

22. 'Non-industrial' inputs include repairs and maintenance; hire of plant and machinery; licensing of vehicles; rates; postage; telephone, etc; advertising market research; professional services; royalties; insurance premia. These we have regarded as overheads and have not deducted them from sales revenue.

23. See, for example, 'Capital Utilisation in Manufacturing Industry', *Bank of England Quarterly Bulletin*, December 1971, from whence the estimates for 1955—64 are taken. A linear relationship between a seventeen-quarter moving average of output and capital stock was shown to fit 'very well'.

24. These industries were the few cases where a direct estimate of capacity utilisation over an extended time horizon was available.

25. The level of vacancies in 1973 and 1974 looks a little odd, but perhaps since the vacancy statistics are not hard statistics we should not be too surprised by a few odd results. If production rates are sharply revised upwards from an initial low level, it is quite likely that employers will overstate their level of vacancies in the scramble to hire workers. It is significant to note that only at the peak of the 1973—4 mini-boom did shortages of skilled labour rank as the most important factor limiting output in the CBI surveys of factors constraining output which ran from 1963 onwards.

26. This of course is still not a complete measure of non-pecuniary managerial income. Much of the expenditure which determines managerial utility would not be counted as fringe benefits by the tax authorities. This would apply essentially to all managerial consumption activities within the corporation — such things as more opulent offices, a bigger and more attractive staff, a more prestigious office address, conferences in Bermuda or St Moritz, etc.

27. Two specific points are made: (a) company cars are being increasingly provided for employees earning less than £8500 p.a. and (b) the practice of companies paying for employees private motoring (including petrol and servicing) is rapidly increasing.

28. A paper by Elliot and Fallick (1979), purporting to show salary growth falling behind the growth in wages, is misleading in two respects. First, the differential incidence of non-pecuniary benefits is never commented on, and second, the coverage of the salary series is extremely restrictive — total reliance is placed on *Historical Salaries* (1968), published by NALGO, and unspecified 'information from employers' organisations and trade unions.' A footnote records that the salary data refer to public sector, non-manual employees, but the clear impression given is that the result obtained is perfectly general.

29. We are assuming that the non-pecuniary income of wage earners is much less important and either cannot, or will not, be increased very rapidly over time. There are of course times and circumstances when employers will be interested in paying workers in a form such that the effective rate of tax is lower, but such circumstances will be very much restricted. It is also the case that employers will want to use incomes policies as justification for paying less.

30. For engineering, whilst the salariat (managerial, scientific, technical and clerical) increased its share of the labour force by about 20 per cent between 1964 and 1972, managers increased their share by about 27 per cent.

31. The actual magnitude of the ratio M/W has a very specific meaning. It relates to the ratio of these costs for the average establishment and not to the ratio of the cost of materials coming into the manufacturing sector from outside sources to wage costs for the manufacturing sector.

32. In an interesting appendix to the article by Clark and Williams (1978), N. H. Jenkinson has attempted to explain the variation in

the share of real profits over time by reference to short-term cost changes, capacity utilisation and a time trend. However, rather severe specification problems indicate that further work is needed before any results obtained would justify close attention.

33. There are conflicting results on this, with Feldstein and Summers (1977) and Holland and Myers (1978) concluding that there is no trend, whereas Nordhaus (1974) and Weisskopf (1979) discern some downward trend. However, Holland and Myers show fairly clearly that the Nordhaus interpretation is at fault, and the Weisskopf estimates show only a very small trend.

34. Certainly this view has been convincingly articulated: see Williamson (1970).

35. He actually examines the period 1949(IV) through 1975(I), and the first and last cycles appear more in line with the 'exhaustion of the reserve army predictions; i.e. the initial source of decline was a rise in the share of wages.

References

Aaronovitch, S. and Sawyer, M. (1975) *Big Business: Theoretical and Empirical Aspects of Concentration and Mergers in the UK*, London, Macmillan.

Armour, H. O. and Teece, D. J. (1978) 'Organisational Structure and Economic Performance: A Test of the Multidivisional Hypothesis', *Bell Journal of Economics*.

Bain, J. S (1956) *Barriers to New Competition*, Cambridge, Mass., Harvard University Press.

Baran, P. 1957) *The Political Economy of Growth*, New York, Monthly Review Press.

Baran, P. and Sweezy, P. (1966) *Monopoly Capital*, New York, Monthly Review Press.

Barbee, W. C. (1974) 'An Inquiry into the Relationship between Market Concentration and Labor's Share of Value Added', Ph.D. Dissertation, Catholic University of America.

Baumol, W. J. (1967) *Business Behavior, Value and Growth*, New York, Harcourt Brace Jovanovitch.

Benham, L. (1972) 'The Effect of Advertising on the Price of Eyeglasses', *Journal of Law and Economics*, October.

Blattner, N. (1972) 'Domestic Competition and Foreign Trade: The Case of the Excess Capacity Barrier to Entry', *Zeitschrift für Nationalökonomie*.

Bothwell, J. L. and Keeler, J. E. (1976) 'Profits, Market Structure and Portfolio Risk', in Masson, R. T. and Qualls, P. D. (eds), *Essays on Industrial Organization in Honor of Joe S. Bain*, Cambridge, Mass., Ballinger.

Boyer, K. (1974) 'Informative and Goodwill Advertising', *Review of Economics and Statistics*, November.

Brack, J. and Cowling, K. (1980) 'Advertising and Hours of Work in US Manufacturing 1919–75', *Warwick Economic Research Paper*, no. 178, September.

Braverman, L. (1974) *Labor and Monopoly Capital: The Degradation of Work in the Twentieth Century*, New York, Monthly Review Press.

Bronfenbrenner, M. (1950) 'Wages in Excess of Marginal Revenue Product', *Southern Economic Journal*, January.

Brown, W. and Terry, M. (1978) 'The Changing Nature of National Wage Agreements', *Scottish Journal of Political Economy*, June.

Burkitt, B. and Bowers, D. (1979) *Trade Unions and the Economy*, London, Macmillan.

Burman, J. P. (1970) 'Capacity Utilization and the Determinants of Fixed Investment', in Holton, K. and Heathfield, D. F. (eds), *The Econometric Study of the UK*, London, Macmillan.

Burmeister, E. and Taubman, P. (1969) 'Labour and Non-Labour Income Saving Propensities', *Canadian Journal of Economics*.

Cable, J. (1972) 'Market Structure, Advertising Policy and Intermarket Differences in Advertising Intensity', in Cowling, K. (ed.), *Market Structure and Corporate Behaviour*, London, Gray-Mills.

Channon, D. (1973) *The Strategy and Structure of British Enterprise*, Cambridge, Mass., Harvard University Press.

Chandler, A. D. and Daems, H. (1974) 'The Rise of Managerial Capitalism and its Impact on Investment Strategy', Working Paper, European Institute for Advanced Studies in Management, Brussels.

Chemicals EDC (1971) *Investment in the Chemicals Industry*, London, NEDO.

Chenery, H. B. (1952) 'Overcapacity and the Acceleration Principle', *Econometrica*, January.

Clark, J. A. and Williams, N. P. (1978) 'Measures of Real Profitability', *Bank of England Quarterly Bulletin*, December.

Clough, R. (1978) 'Capital Investment in the UK', mimeo, CIEBR, University of Warwick.

Comanor, W. S. and Wilson, T. A. (1967) 'Advertising,

Market Structure and Performance', *Review of Economics and Statistics,* November.

Cowling, K. (1976) 'On the Theoretical Specification of Industrial Structure—Performance Relationships', *European Economic Review.*

Cowling, K. (1978a) 'Monopoly, Welfare and Distribution', in Artis, M. and Nobay, R. (eds), *Contemporary Economic Analysis,* London, Croom Helm.

Cowling, K. (1978b) 'Monopolies and Mergers Policy: A View on the Green Paper', *Warwick Economic Research Paper,* November.

Cowling, K., Cable, J., Kelly, M. and McGuinness, T. (1975) *Advertising and Economic Behaviour,* London, Macmillan.

Cowling, K. and Cubbin, J. (1972) 'Hedonic Price Indexes for Cars in the UK', *Economic Journal,* September.

Cowling, K., Dean, M., Wabe, S. and Pyatt, G. (1968) 'An Investigation into the Demand for Manpower and its Supply in the Engineering Industries', CIEBR Research Paper No. 1, University of Warwick.

Cowling, K. and Molho, I. (1980) 'Wage Share, Concentration and Unionism', paper given at the Conference of the European Association for Research in Industrial Economics, Milan, September.

Cowling, K., Stoneman, P., Cubbin, J., Cable, T., Hall, G., Domberger, S. and Dutton, P. (1980) *Mergers and Economic Performance,* Cambridge, Cambridge University Press.

Cowling, K. and Waterson, M. (1976) 'Price—Cost Margins and Market Structure', *Economica,* May.

Crosland, C. A. R. (1962) *The Conservative Enemy,* London, Cape.

Cubbin, J. (1975a) 'Quality Change and Pricing Behaviour in the UK Car Industry 1956—1968', *Economica,* February.

Cubbin, J. (1975b) 'Apparent Collusion, Price—Cost Margins and Advertising in Oligopoly', mimeo.

Cubbin, J. and Leech, D. (1980) 'On the Size of Controlling Shareholding', *Warwick Economic Research Paper,* no. 168.

Demsetz, H. (1973) *The Market Concentration Doctrine,* Washington, D.C., The American Enterprise Institute.

Dixit, A. (1979) 'A Model of Duopoly Suggesting a Theory of Entry Barriers', *Bell Journal of Economics,* Spring.

Dixit, A. (1980) 'The Role of Investment in Entry Deterrence', *Economic Journal*, March.

Duesenberry, J. S. (1967) *Income, Saving and the Theory of Consumer Behavior*, New York, Oxford University Press.

Dunnett, P. (1980) *The Decline of the British Motor Industry*, London, Croom Helm.

Dutton, P. (1976) 'The Impact of Government Competition Policy, Imports and Tariffs on Price—Cost Margins for British Manufacturing Industries', CIEBR, University of Warwick, Discussion Paper 65.

Eichner, A. S. (1976) *The Megacorp and Oligopoly*, Cambridge, Cambridge University Press.

Elliott, R. F. and Fallick, J. L. (1979) 'Pay Differentials in Perspective: A Note on Manual and Non-Manual Pay over the Period 1951—75', *Economic Journal*, June.

Elliott, R. F. and Steele, R. (1976) 'The Importance of National Agreements', *British Journal of Industrial Relations*.

Feldstein, M. and Summers, L. (1977) 'Is the Rate of Profit Falling?', *Brookings Papers on Economic Activity*.

Ferguson, C. (1969) *The Neoclassical Theory of Production and Distribution*, Cambridge, Cambridge University Press.

Fisher, F. M., Griliches, Z. and Kaysen, C. (1962) 'The Costs of Automobile Model Changes since 1949', *Journal of Political Economy*, October.

Friedman, A. L. (1977) *Industry and Labour: Class Struggle at Work and Monopoly Capitalism*, London, Macmillan.

Gaskins, D. W. (1971) 'Dynamic Limit Pricing: Optimal Pricing under Threat of Entry', *Journal of Economic Theory*.

Geroski, P. A. (1981) 'Specification and Testing the Profits—Concentration Relationship: Some Experiments for the UK', *Economica*.

Geroski, P. A., Hamlin, A. P. and Knight, K. G. (1980) 'Wages, Bargaining Power and Market Structure', *Oxford Economic Papers*.

Glyn, A. and Sutcliffe, B. (1972) *British Capitalism, Workers and the Profits Squeeze*, Harmondsworth, Penguin Books.

Gordon, R. J. (1965) 'Airline Costs and Managerial Efficiency', *Transportation Economics*, New York, Columbia University Press.

Grahl, J. (1979) 'Marxism and International Recession', *Marxism Today*, March.

Gribben, J. D. (1974) 'The Operation of the Mergers Panel since 1965', *Trade and Industry*, 17 January.

Hannah, L. and Kay, J. (1977) *Concentration in Modern Industry*, London, Macmillan.

Harrod, R. (1936) 'Imperfect Competition and the Trade Cycle', *Review of Economic Statistics*, February.

Hart, P. E. and Morgan, E. (1977) 'Market Structure and Economic Performance in the UK', *Journal of Industrial Economics*, March.

Hazledine, T. (1978) 'Distribution, Efficiency and Market Power: A Study of UK Manufacturing Industry 1954—73', Ph.D. Thesis, University of Warwick.

Hazledine, T. (1979a) 'On the Nature of Industrial Market Power in the UK', *Warwick Economic Research Paper*, no. 146.

Hazledine, T. (1979b) 'Generalizing from Case Studies: The First 46 Reports of the UK Price Commission', *Warwick Economic Research Paper*, no. 147.

Hines, A. J. (1964) 'Trade Unions and Wage Inflation in the UK 1893—1961', *Review of Economic Studies*, October.

Hitiris, T. (1978) 'Effective Protection and Economic Performance in UK Manufacturing Industry, 1967 and 1968', *Economic Journal*, March.

Holland, D. M. and Myers, S. C. (1978) 'Trends in Corporate Profitability and Capital Costs', mimeo, Massachusetts Institute of Technology, May.

Holterman, S. (1973) 'Market Structure and Economic Performance in UK Manufacturing Industry', *Journal of Industrial Economics*, no. 20.

Holton, R. H. (1957) 'Price Discrimination at Retail: the Supermarket Case', *Journal of Industrial Economics*.

Hood, W. and Rees, R. D. (1974) 'Inter-industry Wage Levels in UK Manufacturing', *Manchester School*, June.

Houthakker, H. and Taylor, L. (1970) *Consumer Demand in the US 1929—70*, 2nd edn, Cambridge, Mass., Harvard University Press.

Ironmonger, D. S. (1970) *New Commodities and Consumer Behaviour*, Cambridge, Cambridge University Press.

Jacquemin, A. and Cardon, M. (1973) 'Size, Structure, Stability and Performance of the Largest British and EEC Firms', *European Economic Review*, no. 4.

Jacquemin, A. and de Jong, H. (eds) (1976) *Markets, Corporate Behaviour and the State*, The Hague, Nijhoff.

Johnson, H. (1973) *The Theory of Income Distribution*, London, Gray-Mills.

Johnston, J. (1960) *Statistical Cost Analysis*, New York, McGraw-Hill.

Kaldor, N. (1955) 'Alternative Theories of Distribution', *Review of Economic Studies*.

Kalecki, M. (1938) 'Distribution of National Income', *Econometrica*, no. 6.

Kalecki, M. (1939) *Essays in the Theory of Economic Fluctuations*, London, Allen & Unwin.

Kalecki, M. (1971a) *Dynamics of the Capitalist Economy*, Cambridge, Cambridge University Press.

Kalecki, M. (1971b) 'Class Struggle and the Distribution of Income', *Kyklos*, no. 24.

Kamerschen, D. (1968) 'The Influence of Ownership and Control of Profit Rates', *American Economic Review*, June.

Kaysen, C. (1957) 'The Social Significance of the Modern Corporation', *American Economic Review*, May.

Kerr, C. (1957) 'Labor's Income Share and the Labor Movement', Chapter 10 in Taylor, G. W. and Pierson, F. C. (eds), *New Concepts in Wage Determination*, New York, McGraw-Hill.

Khalilzadeh-Shirazi, H. (1974) 'Market Structure and Price–Cost Margins in UK Manufacturing Industries', *Review of Economics and Statistics*, February.

King, M. and Mairesse, J. (1978) 'Profitability in Britain and France (1956–75): A Comparative Study', mimeo, September.

Klein, L. R., Ball, R. J., Hazlewood, A. and Vandome, P. (1961) *An Econometric Model of the United Kingdom*, Oxford, Blackwell.

Klein, L. R. and Goldberger, A. S. (1955) *An Econometric Model of the United States, 1929–52*, Amsterdam, North-Holland.

Knight, A. (1974) *Private Enterprise and Public Intervention,* London, Allen & Unwin.

Lambrinides, M. (1973) 'Private Saving and the Macro-economic Distribution of Income: The Classical and the Managerial Savings Functions', *Warwick Economic Research Paper,* No. 36.

Lambrinides, M. (1974) 'Saving and Social Choice: An Analysis of the Relationship between Corporate and Personal Saving', *Warwick Economic Research Paper,* No. 42.

Larner, R. (1970) *Management and the Large Corporation,* New York, Dunellen.

Levinson, H. M. (1954) 'Collective Bargaining and Income Distribution', *American Economic Review,* May,

Levinson, H. M. (1967) 'Unionism, Concentration and Wage Changes: Towards a Unified Theory', *Industrial and Labor Relations Review,* January,

Lyons, B. (1979a) 'Price—Cost Margins, Market Structure and International Trade', paper presented at AUTE Annual Conference, Exeter.

Lyons, B. (1979b) 'International Trade, Industrial Pricing and Profitability: A Survey', paper presented at the Annual Conference of EARIE, Paris.

Machine Tool EDC (1973) *Industrial Review to 1977,* London, NEDO.

Mancke, R. B. (1974) 'Interfirm Profitability Differences', *Quarterly Journal of Economics,* May.

Mandel, E. (1968) *Marxist Economic Theory,* London, Merlin Press.

Marglin, S. (1974) 'What do Bosses do? The Origins and Functions of Hierarchy in Capitalist Production', *Review of Radical Political Economics,* Summer.

Marris, R. (1964) *The Economic Theory of Managerial Capitalism,* London, Macmillan.

McEachern, W. A. (1975) *Managerial Control and Performance,* New York, Heath & Co.

McGuinness, T. and Cowling, K. (1975) 'Advertising and Aggregate Demand for Cigarettes', *European Economic Review,* April.

Meeks, G. (1977) *Disappointing Marriage: A Study of the Gains from Merger,* Cambridge, Cambridge University Press.

Modigliani, F. (1958) 'New Developments on the Oligopoly Front', *Journal of Political Economy*, June.

Monopolies Commission (1968) *Report on the Supply of Cellulosic Fibres*, London, HMSO.

Monsen, R. T., Chiu, J. S. and Cooley, D. E. (1968) 'The Effect of Separation of Ownership and Control on the Performance of the Large Firm', *Quarterly Journal of Economics*, August.

Moroney, J. R. and Allen, B. T. (1969) 'Monopoly Power and the Relative Share of Labor', *Industrial and Labour Relations Review*, January.

Motor Manufacturing EDC (1970) *Economic Assessment to 1972*, London, NEDO.

Mueller, D. C. (1977) 'The Effects of Conglomerate Mergers', *Journal of Banking and Finance*.

Murfin, A. (1980) 'Savings Propensities from Wage and Non-Wage Income', *Warwick Economic Research Paper*, no. 174.

Neumann, M., Bobel, I. and Haid, A. (1979) 'Profitability, Risk and Market Structure in West German Industries', *Journal of Industrial Economics*, March.

Newbould, G. D. (1970) *Management and Merger Activity*, Liverpool, Guthstead.

Nicholson, M. (1972) *Oligopoly and Conflict*, Liverpool, Liverpool University Press.

Nickell, S. and Metcalf, D. (1978) 'Monopolistic Industries and Monopoly Profits', *Economic Journal*, June.

Nobay, A. R. (1970) 'Forecasting Manufacturing Investment — Some Preliminary Results', *National Institute Economic Review*, May.

Nordhaus, W. D. (1974) 'The Falling Share of Profits', *Brookings Papers on Economic Activity*.

Nordhaus, W. D. and Tobin, J. (1972) 'Is Growth Obsolete?' in *Economic Growth*, New York, NBER.

Pagoulatos, E. and Sorensen, R. (1976) 'Foreign Trade, Concentration and Profitability in Open Economies', *European Economic Review*, January.

Palmer, J. (1973) 'The Profit Performance Effects of the Separation of Ownership from Control in Large US Corporations', *Bell Journal of Economics and Management Science*, Spring.

Panić, M. and Vernon, K. (1975) 'Major Factors behind Investment Decisions in British Manufacturing Industry', *Oxford Bulletin of Economics and Statistics*, August.

Papanek, G. F. (1967) *Pakistan's Development: Social Goals and Private Incentives*, Cambridge, Mass., Harvard University Press.

Peel, D. (1975) 'Advertising and Aggregate Consumption', in Cowling, K. *et al.*, *Advertising and Economic Behaviour*, London, Macmillan.

Peretz, D. (1976) 'Finance for Investment − Issues and Non-Issues', *Banker*, April.

Phillips, A. (1961) 'A Theory of Inter-firm Organization', *Quarterly Journal of Economics*, November.

Pollard, S. (1978) 'Labour in Great Britain', in Mathias, P. and Postan, M. M. (eds), *The Cambridge Economic History of Europe*, Cambridge, Cambridge University Press.

Posner, R. A. (1975) 'The Social Costs of Monopoly and Regulation', *Journal of Political Economy*, August.

Prais, S. J. (1976) *The Evolution of Giant Firms in Britain*, Cambridge, Cambridge University Press.

Quinn, T. K. (1953) *Giant Business: Threat to Democracy*, New York, Cambridge University Press.

Rammos, A. B. (1979) 'Import Competition, Market Structure and Price−Cost Margins', M. A. Dissertation, University of Warwick.

Review of Monopolies and Mergers Policy: A Consultative Document (1978), London, HMSO.

Rhys, D. G. (1972) *The Motor Industry: An Economic Survey*, London, Butterworth.

Rothschild, K. (1942) 'A Note on Advertising', *Economic Journal*, April.

Rowthorn, B. (1979) 'Underconsumption Theories', mimeo.

Rowthorn, B. (1980) *Capitalism, Conflict and Inflation*, London, Lawrence & Wishart.

Rumelt, R. P. (1974) 'Strategy, Structure and Economic Performance', Division of Research, Harvard Graduate School of Business Administration.

Samuels, J. and Smyth, D. (1968) 'Profits, Variability of Profits and Firm Size', *Economica*, May.

Savage, D. (1977) 'A Comparison of Accelerator Models of

Manufacturing Investment', Discussion Paper No. 9, National Institute of Economic and Social Research.

Saving, T. (1970) 'Concentration Ratios and the Degree of Monopoly', *International Economic Review*.

Scherer, F. M. (1980) *Industrial Market Structure and Economic Performance*, 2nd edn, Chicago, Rand McNally.

Select Committee on Science and Technology (1971) *The Prospects for the United Kingdom Computer Industry in the 1970s*, 4th Report, Vol. II 'Minutes of Evidence', London, HMSO.

Simon, H. A. (1957) 'The Compensation of Executives', *Sociometry*, March.

Simon, J. (1970) *Issues in the Economics of Advertising*, Urbana, University of Illinois Press.

Singh, A. (1971) *Takeovers*, Cambridge, Cambridge University Press.

Skidelsky, R. (ed.) (1977) *The End of the Keynesian Era*, London, Macmillan.

Smyth, D. J. and Briscoe G. (1971) 'Investment and Capacity Utilisation in the UK 1923–66', *Oxford Economic Papers*, March.

Spence, M. (1977) 'Entry, Investment and Oligopolistic Pricing', *Bell Journal of Economics*, Autumn.

Steer, P. (1978) 'Organizational Form and Firm Performance: An Analysis of the Structure of Large UK Companies', Ph.D. Thesis, University of Warwick.

Steer, P. and Cable, J. (1978) 'Internal Organization and Profit: An Empirical Analysis of Large UK Companies', *Journal of Industrial Economics*, September.

Stein, H. (1969) *The Fiscal Revolution in America*, Chicago, Chicago University Press.

Steindl, J. (1952) *Maturity and Stagnation in American Capitalism*, Oxford, Oxford University Press.

Steinherr, A. and Thisse, J. (1979) 'Are Labor-Managers Really Perverse?', *Economic Letters*.

Stigler, G. (1964) 'A Theory of Oligopoly', *Journal of Political Economy*, February.

Stonebraker, R. J. (1976) 'Corporate Profits and the Risk of Entry', *Review of Economics and Statistics*, February.

Sweezy, P. (1939) 'Demand under Conditions of Oligopoly', *Journal of Political Economy*, August.

Sylos-Labini, P. (1962) *Oligopoly and Technical Progress*, Cambridge, Mass., Harvard University Press.

Taylor, C. T. (1978) 'Why is Britain in Recession?', *Bank of England Quarterly Bulletin*, March.

Taylor, L. D. and Weiserbs, D. (1972) 'Advertising and the Aggregate Consumption Function', *American Economic Review*, September.

Taylor, J., Winter, D. and Pearce, D. (1970) 'A 19 Industry Quarterly Series of Capacity Utilisation in the UK 1948–68', *Oxford Bulletin of Economics and Statistics*.

Thompson, A. W. J., Mulvey, C. and Farbman, M. (1977) 'Bargaining Structure and Relative Earnings in GB', *British Journal of Industrial Relations*.

Tullock, G. (1967) 'The Welfare Costs of Tariffs, Monopolies and Theft', *Western Economic Journal*, June.

Utton, M. (1969) 'Diversification, Mergers and Profitability', *Business Ratios*.

Utton, M. (1974) 'On Measuring the Effects of Industrial Mergers', *Scottish Journal of Political Economy*.

Vanek, J. (1970) *The General Theory of Labour Managed Market Economies*, Ithaca, Cornell University Press.

Warren-Boulton, F. (1974) 'Vertical Control with Variable Proportions', *Journal of Political Economy*, July–August.

Waterson, M. (1976) 'Price–Cost Margins and Market Structure', Ph.D. Thesis, University of Warwick.

Waterson, M. (1980) 'Price–Cost Margins and Successive Market Power', *Quarterly Journal of Economics*, February.

Weiss, L. (1966) 'Concentration and Labor Earnings', *American Economic Review*, March.

Weiss, L. (1971) 'Quantitative Studies of Industrial Organization', in Intriligator, M. (ed.), *Frontiers of Quantitative Economics*, Amsterdam, North-Holland.

Weiss, L. (1974) 'The Concentration–Profits Relationship and Antitrust' in Goldschmid, H., Mann, H. and Weston, J. F. (eds), *Industrial Concentration: The New Learning*, Boston, Little, Brown.

Weisskopf, T. D. (1979) 'Marxian Crisis Theory and the Rate

of Profit in the Post-war US Economy', *Cambridge Journal of Economics*, December.

Weitzman, M. L. (1974) 'Prices vs. Quantities', *Review of Economic Studies*, October.

Whitley, J. D. (1979) 'Imports of Finished Manufactures: The Effects of Prices, Demand and Capacity', *Manchester School*, December.

Whittington, G. (1980) 'The Profitability and Size of United Kingdom Companies, 1960–74', *Journal of Industrial Economics*, June.

Williams, N. (1979) 'The Profitability of UK Industrial Sectors', *Bank of England Quarterly Bulletin*, December.

Williamson, O. E. (1964) *The Economics of Discretionary Behavior: Managerial Objectives in a Theory of the Firm*, Englewood Cliffs, Prentice-Hall.

Williamson, O. E. (1965) 'A Dynamic Theory of Inter-firm Behavior', *Quarterly Journal of Economics*, November.

Williamson, O. E. (1970) *Corporate Control and Business Behavior: An Inquiry into the Effects of Organization Form and Enterprise Behavior*, Englewood Cliffs, Prentice-Hall.

Yancey, T. (1958) 'Some Effects of Quality and Selling Effort in a Dynamic Macroeconomic Model', Ph.D. Dissertation, University of Illinois.

Index